generosity

generosity
big-heartedness as a way of life

michael wakely

Inter-Varsity Press

Inter-Varsity Press
38 De Montfort Street, Leicester LE1 7GP, England
Email: ivp@uccf.org.uk
Website: www.ivpbooks.com

First published 2004

British Library Cataloguing-in-Publication Data
A catalogue record for this book is available from the British Library.

ISBN 1–84474–020–x

Set in Monotype Dante 10.5/13pt

Typeset in Great Britain by Servis Filmsetting Ltd, Manchester
Printed and bound in Great Britain by Creative Print and Design (Wales),
Ebbw Vale

*Inter-Varsity Press is the publishing division of the Universities and
Colleges Christian Fellowship (formerly the Inter-Varsity Fellowship), a
student movement linking Christian Unions in universities and colleges
throughout Great Britain, and a member movement of the International
Fellowship of Evangelical Students. For more information about local
and national activities write to UCCF, 38 De Montfort Street, Leicester
LE1 7GP, email us at email@uccf.org.uk, or visit the UCCF website at
www.uccf.org.uk.*

Contents

Foreword

We live in an ephemeral age, when news is delivered in sound-bites, celebrities are listened to more than politicians and stories require 'spin'. The media are dominated by an alluring combination of fame, celebrity and publicity. And it's a 'must-have' material world, with designer goods, fast food and junk mail. Success has become quintessentially about glamour, hype and branding. You are what you have.

Yet the inequalities of our global village are sobering. We spend more on pet food every year than the amount needed to cover basic nutrition and health for every person on the planet. Americans annually shell our four times as much on cosmetics than the estimated cost of giving everyone in the world a basic education.

Sometimes, we respond in a 'quick fix' manner: we reach for the cheque book following an emotive appeal or respond to a charity telethon, dial the free 0800 number, and punch in our credit-card details. We expect our donation to solve the problem, and we become curiously detached. But there is a more considered and ongoing role for us to play as generous global citizens with our brothers and sisters in the worldwide family of God.

If you're caught between your culture and your faith, *Generosity* is for you. Mike Wakely has written a timeless, back-to-basics, no-nonsense, common-sense book that pulsates with the conviction of a man who has lived the life he is talking about.

Generosity is written with confidence and candour. It won't try to tell you what to do or substitute the author's judgment for your own. Instead it gently reminds us of the generous heart of God, who lets us call him Father, and inspires us to fashion ourselves into the 'family likeness'.

Mike challenges the materialism, so prevalent even in the church today, with his own style of 'extra-mile living'. Packed with razor-sharp anecdotes, he reminds us about the practical ways we can share all that we have been given, and reveals just how enriching and rewarding the experience of giving can be. His useful study notes both deepen and extend the scope of this valuable book.

Mike Wakely dusts away any doubts you ever had about living out your faith in a consumer generation, and gives practical expression to the deep, ancient truths of Scripture.

I suspect that this book will be remembered as a turning point for those who draw close and allow its message to transform their experience.

DANNY SMITH
*Director of Jubilee Action and of the Jubilee Campaign,
and Editor of* Just Right

Introduction

In the summer of 2000 I met up with an old friend, an Indian Christian leader whom I had not seen for twenty-five years. That length of time makes a big difference. I remembered Pran as a young man with a thin face and a healthy crop of hair on his head. It took some time to recognize the middle-aged, balding gentleman who introduced himself. No doubt he had the same difficulty with me. But his smile was the same, his voice, his memories.

'Do you remember the old man in Bilgram?' he asked, in mid-conversation.

Do I remember? Indeed! How could I ever forget?

Pran and I had been travelling in the same evangelistic team in northern India in 1970. Five or six young men, we went from village to village in a large delivery van, stopping to preach through a loudspeaker and to sell Gospels and other Christian books to the huge crowds that gathered everywhere to hear us. Today the Indian State of Uttar Pradesh would be the fifth-largest country in the world if it were an independent nation.[1] In fact it is just one political division of India. Almost all of its inhabitants are either Hindu or Muslim. Only one-tenth of 1% profess to be Christian.

One day we arrived at a small village called Bilgram (you won't find it on any but the largest-scale map), opened up the back of our truck and began to preach our gospel message. As we started to sell the Scriptures, an old man accosted us, a broad smile lighting up his face.

'You must come to my home,' he insisted.

When our work was done and we had sold the books people wanted to buy, we gathered and followed the old man to his home.

Home was a simple, one-room, mud and brick building, the epitome of simplicity and poverty. There he lived with his wife and several children, eking out his existence on a daily labouring wage. Furniture was limited to a rough bed, some pots and pans and a few other simple things.

Poverty personified. And yet our host welcomed us like royalty, sat us down on the bed and wherever else there was a space to sit, brought us tea and insisted we stay for a meal. Seeing how poor he was, we tried hard to resist. We couldn't stay; we had to move on. But nothing would change his mind.

This man and his small family were Christians, the only Christians in Bilgram and probably the only Christians for many miles. And he was not going to allow the moment to pass without serving us and lavishing his best on us. We were clearly the greatest cause for joy to pass through his small home for a long time.

He had only a few chickens, scratching about in the dust outside (and inside) his door, but one of them went into the pot that day. And as we ate this royal meal, the old man and his family sat watching us feast at his table. Happiness was written on their faces.

We left Bilgram later that evening, very humbled by the graphic picture of Christian love and moved by the generosity of one who had so little to give, but gave it all with joy.

Over many years I have been on the receiving end of a lot of generosity and kindness, and I hope I have passed on my share. In the life of the old man in Bilgram we saw generosity overflowing from a very big heart, and that is the virtue I want to celebrate here – a quality that is much more than giving away money or possessions (but one that cannot be achieved without doing that). It springs from a heart that has been touched by the greatest of all givers, God himself.

This book is dedicated to that old man and his family who lived in Bilgram, Uttar Pradesh, India, but whose names are surely inscribed in the Lamb's Book of Life. I want his testimony to touch the lives of another generation.

1

The heart of a father

My father died when I was only two years old, as a result of a car accident. He was a gold-medallist in law at Dublin University, won the Military Cross for bravery in France in 1917 and then joined the Colonial Service in the British West Indies. When war broke out in 1939 he was in service as a magistrate in Jamaica. Because of restrictions on travel, our family lived there until the war was over. My father worked very hard. One day he fell asleep at the wheel. His car went off the road down a small embankment close to home and he died a few days later. That was in 1943.

I have no memories of my father except what my mother told me about him. They had had a short but happy marriage. I grew up feeling that he had been a very good man and that I had been deprived of someone very special.

Growing up without a father meant that I sought father figures elsewhere. The most obvious was my Uncle Henry, my mother's older brother. Uncle Henry had been a Scout master and, during a Scout camp, had faced the awful trauma of fire in a tent, in which several boys had died. The effects of this tragedy had driven him to seek ordination and he became a vicar in the Church of

England. When we came to know him on our return to England after the end of the war, he lived in a large, rambling vicarage in a village with the delightful name of Ducklington, near Witney in Oxfordshire. Mother used to take us to stay with him during school holidays. My brother and I would explore the large gardens, the vicarage's numerous rooms and especially its attic under the eaves, which contained intriguing mysteries – not least boxes of moth-eaten rabbit fur from one of Uncle Henry's early business ventures.

Uncle Henry was one of my father-substitute figures. I probably owe more of my understanding of God than I realize to my childhood memories of Ducklington rectory life. He was the epitome of a rural country vicar, replete with Mothers Union flower shows, a library that contained complete editions of *Punch*, and a fine peal of church bells that rang out on Sundays to call the faithful to Matins. I was occasionally allowed to play tunes on the old church organ, but never to touch the bell-ropes, being warned that I was too light and they would probably pull me off the ground. Uncle Henry was large, rotund and bald, and passionately interested in church architecture.

There was another figure in my childhood to whom I owe even more in my understanding of fatherhood: the awe-inspiring Mr Whicker.

Rolf Whicker was the headmaster of the boys' private prep school my brother and I attended after we graduated from kindergarten. He was a large man with a deep voice that commanded instant respect, if not fear, in his students. His dominant figure stood in astonishing contrast to his small and motherly wife, Kathleen. There was no doubting that behind the great man was the tender influence of his petite wife, and together they oversaw the work of Hillside School.

Mr Whicker's presence dominated the establishment. He led morning prayers, made all the major decisions in staffing and running the school, taught a number of subjects to the upper classes, umpired cricket and refereed football and hockey matches.

Although he was not omnipresent his influence was felt everywhere. His study was on the top floor of the school building, a spacious dwelling that has, sadly, been demolished. To be called to see Mr Whicker in his study would fill us with dread – perhaps an early indication of the meaning of holiness to our young minds. It was usually punishment enough just to be summoned to see him. In reality, he was a kind and patient man who rarely raised his voice in anger.

Mr Whicker was also my history and Latin teacher. He introduced me to Caesar's *Gallic Wars* and to *amo, amas, amat*. Woe betide me if I forgot my tenses! He also taught Scripture. His powerful voice contributed to an annual performance of the local Gilbert and Sullivan operatic society, and each year the whole school trooped down to the town to watch *The Pirates of Penzance* or *The Gondoliers*, in which he sang a leading part.

Mr Whicker was one of my most significant and influential father figures, and no doubt a father figure to generations of schoolboys who studied at Hillside School. I quickly grew to respect his stern image and firm discipline and to formulate my regard for authority from them.

Then I discovered his private and remarkable generosity.

After the war, my mother had returned to England as a widow in considerable poverty. She had two sons to care for but no job and little cash in the bank. Somehow she came to know Mr Whicker and his school and he offered her a teaching job. More than that, realizing her difficult situation, he offered free education in the school to my brother and me. Rolf and Kathleen Whicker provided protection and security for us and for many who came close to his gentle and kind influence.

Firm in discipline, stern in appearance, requiring respect – and yet at heart gentle and patient, slow to anger and very big-hearted. This gave me my early insights into the Father figure who has dominated my life – the biblical person of God, the Father, after whom all fatherhood is named.

The reality behind the shadow

The image of my old headmaster is only a pale reflection of the true nature of my Father in heaven, but it is at least a pale reflection. God was never a severe authority figure living in awesome isolation in his bare study, because he was never solitary or isolated and his environment was never bare. He did not need a universe of creatures to prove his dominance or to keep him company. His school had no students, but his house was not empty. Within the mystery of his uniqueness the Father spoke and he loved his Word. He commissioned his Spirit and sent him out to accomplish his will. Like a family they had one another, Father, Son and Spirit, one God, complete, together and unique.

There are mysteries in God that we can only grasp at and guess at, but there are also certain fixed qualities that are absolutely clear and unambiguous. One is his principled nature: he is a God of order and righteousness, and everything he does is by definition good. Another is his extraordinary quality of love. Hatred and all its ugly derivatives – selfishness, jealousy, the will to hurt and harm – are alien to him. Alongside his stern commitment to law and order is a passionate love that craves companionship and all the values that give birth to relationship.

So there was God, a triune unity, bound together by love. Everything he owned, which was everything, was owned in common within the family. Giving and sharing together, the triune God ruled. What a picture of harmony and creative power!

More extraordinary still (I hope my imagination is not stretching too far), that craving for companionship and relationship overflowed into creation. In a burst of expressive energy, not wanting to keep his pleasure and glory to himself, God's qualities of love and generosity – his big-heartedness – led him to make creatures that would benefit from and enjoy his nature.

It began with a dazzling cosmic firework display. God is Light, and perhaps that is why he began his creation with light in imitation of his glory. Then he moved on to the building-blocks of a universe – material objects such as the Earth and the planets, the stars and the heavens, essential structures for its future inhabitants. In his creative imagination he turned to the finer details, starting to fashion the Earth and to prepare it for occupation. The house was equipped with furniture. We need only look around at the world to see what a fine craftsman he was. And finally, when all was ready, and there was dry land and sea, day and night, fruit and vegetation, he made animals to inhabit this new world. He filled the sky with birds, the sea with fish and the land with animals.

His greatest invention was still to come. This was what God had prepared everything for – to create human beings, the centre-piece of his heart's desire. 'Let us make man in our image,' he said, '... and let them rule ... over all the earth' (Gen. 1:26). And then, since God saw that the man was not complete all alone, but needed to belong to a family, he made a woman to be Adam's companion.

Creation was the impressive display of a supremely lavish and generous Benefactor with a sensational imagination. Selfishness and greed found no place either in his character or in his creation. It was all done for the benefit of others – for the enjoyment of the creatures and people who now inhabit the universe.

God gave a garden

The creation story is foundational to our understanding not only of God's big-heartedness but also of our relationship to him. The ugly twist in the tale – Adam and Eve's rebellion – is the key that makes sense of the disharmony that has arisen in God's beautiful world, its suffering and sorrow, its tragedies and torture – and that gave rise to the call for redemption and rescue. From the start it was a question of ownership and authority. Who owned this most splendid of God's gifts? And who was in charge?

Adam and Eve challenged God's ownership, rather in the same manner as all revolutionaries who have decided to overthrow established authorities and take over. First Eve and then her man, under the influence of a dark force in the shape of a serpent, decided to challenge God's authority and rewrite the rules. It is an astonishing tale and would have made sensational drama if it had not had such tragic consequences.

The important lesson to grasp is this: the right to human dignity, personal property and freedom belongs to God and has been given to us for our benefit as long as we need it. He is the supreme authority and generous benefactor of us all. In spite of the fall – rebellion and theft by another word – God is still the true owner and the rightful authority. The American Declaration of Independence of 1776 displays real insight when it states: 'We hold these truths to be self-evident, that all men are created equal, that they are endowed by their Creator with certain unalienable Rights, that among these are Life, Liberty and the pursuit of Happiness.'

The Universal Declaration of Human Rights,[1] in its affirmation that 'recognition of the inherent dignity and of the equal and in-alienable rights of all members of the human family is the foundation of freedom, justice and peace in the world', makes sense only under God. That is the lesson of Genesis. We owe everything to the immense generosity of the one we have abused so badly. Woe betide us if we forget to whom it belongs and who gave it to us.

The supreme example

Of course, creation is just the beginning. The history of God's people throughout the Old Testament continues the tale of God's magnanimity. Even as they rejected his laws, lusted after manmade idols and revelled in their greed, God watched over his people and met their needs. At times he might have appeared very stern, but his severity was always geared towards his beloved's best interests and welfare.

And then we come to the culmination of his love. Jesus' parable of the tenants tells it all.

> 'A man planted a vineyard, rented it to some farmers and went away … At harvest time he sent a servant … But the tenants beat him … He sent another servant, but that one also they beat … He sent still a third, and they wounded him and threw him out.
>
> 'Then the owner of the vineyard said, "What shall I do? I will send my son, whom I love; perhaps they will respect him"' (Luke 20:9–13).

'God so loved the world that he gave his one and only Son,' wrote the apostle John (John 3:16). God proved his love by this act of generosity, in this case the supreme gift of a personal sacrifice, the ultimate offering. 'Thanks be to God for his indescribable gift!' said Paul to the Corinthians (2 Cor. 9:15), his imagination stretched and his emotions stirred by God's astonishing magnanimity towards humankind. The amazing truth is that God did all this for people who had rebelled against him, insulted his majesty and broken his laws. As a magnanimous sovereign he reached out in love to those who rejected him.

Generosity to the hostile

Sadly, the true meaning of grace has been lost to everyday usage, a loss that deprives us of one of the most important words in the Christian faith. 'For it is by grace you have been saved, through faith' (Eph. 2:8). What does it really mean?

We say the 'grace' (or, more often, we *don't* say the grace) in order to thank God for our food. We refer to 'his Grace the Archbishop' as a relic of past dignity. And we think wistfully of the 'three Graces' – sister Greek goddesses, givers of charm and beauty, and relatives of the nine Muses, who presided over song and poetry. And so the true meaning of grace drifts from our grasp.

Simply stated, grace means 'getting what we never deserved' – in fact, far more than we could ever have merited or earned, free and independent of our own worth or value. Grace affirms that God gives even to those who deserve the scrap heap, even to those who despise or ignore him. It is easy to imagine a God who gives gifts to those who have earned them, like a successful employer handing out the wages or Father Christmas giving toys to good children. But the God of the Bible gives free gifts to people who don't deserve them! That is biblical grace.

Jesus was in the home of Simon, a wealthy Pharisee, when an extraordinary thing happened. A local prostitute broke into the room, approached, sobbing, behind him and started to pour perfume, mingled with tears, on his feet. It must have been enormously embarrassing for Jesus' host, who was not used to emotional outbursts from street women at his parties, and he evidently didn't know how to respond. So Jesus had time to tell a story.

'Two men owed money to a certain money-lender. One owed him five hundred denarii [about a year's salary], and the other fifty. Neither of them had the money to pay him back, so he cancelled the debts of both. Now which of them will love him more?' (Luke 7:41–42).

The answer is obvious, and the application to the bizarre behaviour of the prostitute just as clear. She had come from the gutter and found acceptance at the feet of Jesus. She had encountered God's extraordinary generosity.

The apostle Paul was no less overcome every time he was reminded of his past as a persecutor and murderer of Christians, and grace is a recurring theme in all his writings. For example: '[God] has saved us and called us to a holy life – not because of anything we have done but because of his own purpose and grace' (2 Tim. 1:9).

John Newton, writer of the hymn 'Amazing Grace', died in 1807 after a long life in which he was transformed from blaspheming slave-trader to prominent preacher of the grace of God. A marble plaque at St Mary Woolnoth Church, Lombard Street, in London, carried the epitaph that Newton himself wrote:

JOHN NEWTON, Clerk
Once an infidel and libertine,
A servant of slaves in Africa,
Was, by the rich mercy of our Lord and Saviour
JESUS CHRIST,
restored, pardoned, and appointed to preach
the Gospel which he had long laboured to destroy.

Christian history is the story of grace, the record of God's unending generosity in reaching down to the gutters and the slums to rescue and restore lost and hopeless humanity. The greater the crime, the greater the gratitude when that crime is pardoned. The deeper the darkness, the brighter shines the glory of grace. 'For you know the grace of our Lord Jesus Christ,' writes Paul, 'that though he was rich, yet for your sakes he became poor, so that you through his poverty might become rich' (2 Cor. 8:9).

That is the nature of the God who has revealed himself to us through the Scriptures and in the person of Jesus Christ. That is where the topic of generosity originates, and that is where we too must begin as we explore this most attractive of Christian values.

His love has no limit, His grace has no measure,
His power has no boundary known unto men;
For out of His infinite riches in Jesus
He giveth, and giveth, and giveth again![2]

2

The fruit of the tree

I was walking through the streets of London when someone beckoned to me from a car that had pulled up by the curb. I thought he was lost and wanted directions, so I went over to him. I bent down and asked if I could help.

'I am Italian,' he said. 'I am coming from an exhibition in Earl's Court and am on my way to the airport. I am a representative of Gucci and I have some Gucci clothes left over from the exhibition. I am looking for someone to give them to.'

Beside him on the seat was a bag in which several items of new clothing were visible, neatly packed in cellophane wrapping. I am not a connoisseur of clothing, but even I have heard of Gucci. I had difficulty knowing how to relate to what he was saying.

'I have no money,' I finally replied. 'And I don't need any new clothes.'

At best, that was a half-truth. I was tempted by the lure of a free deal. I eyed the pile of quality clothing and wondered what my wife would think if I arrived home with a new Gucci shirt and tie.

'No, no,' he insisted, 'I want to give them to you free. I am like Jesus.'

'I don't really believe your offer,' I replied. 'People don't just give away expensive gifts to strangers. There must be some catch. What do you want from me?'

The offer was of course too good to be true, though I never fully understood what the catch was. He refused to allow me to handle the clothes, but wanted me to get into the car so that he could show them to me. This I was not willing to do. Maybe he was a smart operator or a kidnapper – or one of those 'candid camera' TV jokers. Anyway, I didn't believe him, and finally walked away without any Gucci clothing. Totally unconditional free gifts are hard to accept.

What's the catch?

Many people walk away from God's generosity for similar reasons. They just cannot cope with unconditional free offers, even if they come from the Almighty. Somewhere there must be a catch. The mechanics of cause and effect are ingrained into our belief system. Nothing happens without a cause: God will give, if we have done something to attract his attention. Or maybe God will respond to a fair bargain. 'God, save me,' cries the drowning man, 'and I will go to church every week for the rest of my life.'

Some people reject the Christian faith (or endeavour to deny that God exists at all) because they believe the conditions are too harsh. Salvation may indeed be free, but God surely demands that we pay a high price to get it. For others the message is too simple. Religion is a complex subject and a free gift is far too simplistic for our complicated imaginations to grasp. Some find it humiliating to have to acknowledge their dependence upon a charitable donation, and still others just find it too good to be true.

Some years ago I held a serious discussion with a sincere Muslim doctor on the subject of grace. I met him in the southern Pakistani city of Sukkur, where I had called at his private clinic, trying to sell him a Bible. He sat me down and asked me to tell him more. I set out to explain that salvation is a free gift, completely free – for that is what the Bible teaches, and without it we have no hope.

'But that is impossible,' he replied. 'Nothing in life is free. Everything has consequences. For everything there is a price to be paid.' Thus far he was an orthodox Muslim.

'But no,' I insisted. 'If there is a price to be paid for salvation, it is the price of our lives. For that is what we deserve. The Bible is clear that the wages of our sin are death (Rom. 6:23). A righteous God cannot turn a blind eye to crime. Unless God gives us our salvation as a free gift we have no hope.'

'That is immoral and unacceptable,' he countered. 'In Islam we are required and expected to work for our salvation and we get what we deserve. That is righteous and just. If salvation is a free gift, then I can receive it, walk away and do whatever I like. I can go on sinning and still be saved. And that is both unjust and immoral.'

He had stumbled over the very issue that holds the gospel's greatest appeal. What a problem that is to some people! Even the apostle Paul met this argument in his day. 'What shall we say then? Shall we go on sinning, so that grace may increase? By no means! We died to sin; how can we live in it any longer?' (Rom. 6:1–2).

The criminal who has stood in the dock and been fined an impossible sum, or condemned to imprisonment or worse, must surely be a dejected figure. But tell him that a rich benefactor has paid his debts and that he is therefore acquitted and set free, and new horizons open up ahead of him. As he walks from the court as a free man, life takes on a different perspective. Anyone who has received such an undeserved donation should be moved by gratitude and fresh motivation.

Westley Allan Dodd was a convicted serial child-killer, 'a man who had viciously abused and mutilated three young boys, a man who said he would do it again, a man who said there was no hope he would ever be released from the hideous darkness within his soul'.[1] His crimes, committed in Vancouver (USA) in 1989, were premeditated and deliberate and he fully agreed that he deserved to die for what he had done.

Given the traditional opportunity for last words before his execution in Washington State Penitentiary in 1993, Dodd said: 'I was wrong when I said there was no hope, no peace. There is hope. There is peace. I have found both in the Lord Jesus Christ.'

It is reported that witnesses to his execution were furious when they heard this claim to hope coming from the lips of one who so deserved to suffer for his crimes. The father of two of the murdered boys 'hissed quietly' when Dodd invoked the name of Jesus. Is it any surprise, when we are so deeply convinced that we get what we deserve, that at heart we believe there is no such thing as a truly free and undeserved gift? But the gospel proclaims something different.

As sinners, who deserve punishment rather than reward, and condemnation rather than mercy, we too are recipients of God's incredible, undeserved generosity. We have no more earned our salvation than Westley Allan Dodd had. That truth alone should transform us from hostile rebels into grateful subjects, even if Jesus had not also promised the Holy Spirit to oversee and empower the transformation.

There is no catch

There really is no catch. God's salvation is a free and undeserved gift, to be received by faith without works. It is the gift of righteousness in glory in place of rags in the gutter.

At the same time there is an automatic obligation. God's gift grants us a change of status as he welcomes us into his family as his children. 'Now if we are children, then we are heirs – heirs of God and co-heirs with Christ, if indeed we share in his sufferings in order that we may also share in his glory' (Rom. 8:17). It is the obligation to get up out of the gutter and act like royalty.

Now this is a gift far better than a Gucci suit. Yet even if the

A free gift

If you have never understood that this is what grace means, maybe you have never fully thanked God for his gift of salvation through Christ. It is even possible you have never received the free gift of salvation, or been born again into God's family.

Since salvation and the assurance that Christ is your Saviour and Lord do not depend on your virtue or achievement, you have only to put your trust in him and in his forgiveness given through the cross at Calvary in order to be saved. You can pray right now, place your faith in him and ask him to come into your life.

Pray a prayer like this, with all the sincerity of your heart:

Father in heaven,

I thank you that in your love for me you sent your Son Jesus to die on the cross to take away my guilt. I understand that I do not deserve what you have done for me. In fact, I deserve only condemnation for my failure to keep your law. Since salvation is a free gift to be received by faith, however, I now ask you to give me that gift. I put my faith in Christ, and ask you to enter my life by your Holy Spirit, to give me the power to live in gratitude as your disciple and servant.

I pray this prayer, with thanksgiving, in Jesus' name,

Amen.

Gucci offer had been genuine and I had walked away with a bag of expensive new clothes, I would have been under a certain obligation. First, politeness would have required me to thank the donor, and second, as soon as I got home I would have been under obligation to put on my new clothes. I would have joined the Gucci family!

God's free gift is an unbelievable privilege and it carries with it awesome responsibility. Someone has wisely said, 'The entrance fee to heaven is nothing. It is free! But a life-membership subscription costs us everything.' The obligation is the duty of family membership

- to put on my new clothes of righteousness – a new lifestyle
- to develop the family likeness – a new image
- to bear the family name and reputation
- to build the family estate
- to undertake family expectations and responsibilities

Once we grasp this, life can never be the same again. The God of love and grace, the God of generosity and kindness, is developing his likeness in us, and he is doing it by pouring 'his love into our hearts by the Holy Spirit, whom he has given us' (Rom. 5:5).

God loved the world so much that he gave, and we now have the honour of learning to love no less.

The family likeness

Imagine that you have a neighbour who tells you he loves you and cares for you. Every time you see him, he says, 'I am really concerned for you. I like you so much. I care for you. I love you.'

Imagine that one day you fall on hard times. You fall sick. Your other half walks out on you. You lose your job. Your bills mount up so high you have no hope of paying them. Thieves break in and empty your home. What would you expect from your neighbour, who tells you he loves you so much? You would expect him to prove his love by helping you – giving you some money, fetching the doctor, offering his home for you to stay in, or whatever you need. If he did nothing for you, but still said, 'I love you!', you would surely call him a hypocrite, and his words empty and useless.

'Suppose a brother or sister is without clothes and daily food,' says James. 'If one of you says to him, "Go, I wish you well; keep warm and well fed," but does nothing about his physical needs, what good is it?' (James 2:15–16).

We know that God's love was genuine because he proved it to us in sending Jesus into the world. He loved us not just in words (sending us love messages through the prophets) but in painful deeds (at Calvary). If people tell us that they love us, we are within our rights to challenge them: 'If you really love me, prove it!' Love *will* prove itself, if it is genuine.

This is what God did when he saw us raking through the rubbish in desperation. He did not send an 'I love you' message from a distance. He jumped right in and got involved with us, lifting us out of the rubbish pile. If God had not responded, we could rightly have shaken our fists at him. 'Don't talk about love if you don't mean it!' If you want the proof, glance back at Calvary. See the agony, the price he paid that cried out that he did care, that he does love. 'This is how we know what love is: Jesus Christ laid down his life for us' (1 John 3:16).

It is all there in the familiar story of the good Samaritan (Luke 10:30–37). 'A man was going down from Jerusalem to Jericho, when he fell into the hands of robbers. They stripped him of his clothes, beat him and went away, leaving him half-dead.'

After a little while a priest came along the same road. He was a religious professional – dog-collar, robes, prayer book in his hand. He knew the Bible and was familiar with the passage that says, 'Love your neighbour as you love yourself.' But he was busy; he was in a hurry; he had important religious duties to fulfil. So he passed by quickly on the other side of the road.

Some time later, along came another pious person. Maybe he thought he would get dirty if he touched the half-dead body (after all, the Jewish law tells you not to touch a dead body) and that it would be below his station in life to soil his hands. Maybe he thought the poor man needed a doctor rather than a priest. He also passed by quickly and did nothing.

Then a third man arrived. This man was not religious like the others. In fact, Jesus said he belonged to a different class and sect altogether, not at all a member of the established church or of respectable society. He was something of a heretic, unacceptable to good people – a Samaritan. But he didn't just have love in his head. He also had love in his heart, and his instinct was to do something when he saw someone in need: 'and when he saw him, he took pity on him. He went to him and bandaged his wounds, pouring on oil and wine. Then he put the man on his own donkey, brought him to an inn and took care of him.'

That is where the rubber hits the road. And that is the family likeness that the Holy Spirit is working to develop in us.

The ultimate test

Coca Cola has advertised itself across the world as the 'real thing'. What tests can we apply to Coke to know if that is a valid claim? The shape of the bottle? Laboratory examination? Colour or gas quality? Or is it enough just to pour it down our throat to know we have something authentic?

The test of authenticity is a relevant question, because many Christians have taken their salvation for granted without measuring it up against biblical standards. Attending meetings? Enjoying worship experiences? Having a passion to read the Bible and pray? What is it that truly indicates that we have the 'real thing'?

The Bible gives more than one answer to this question. There is the test of the sharpened consciousness of sin, the test of the leading of the Spirit and the test of the witness of the Spirit (Rom.

8:10, 14, 16). There are other tests, and we need to check them out, because it is important to know (though this is not the place to examine all the evidences we should look for).

But here is a significant test, in the heart of the first letter of the apostle John: 'We know that we have passed from death to life, because we love our brothers. Anyone who does not love remains in death' (1 John 3:14).

It is important for everyone who takes Jesus seriously to understand this. We were saved by affirming our faith in the finished work of Christ, and God confirmed it by planting his Holy Spirit in our hearts. After we were saved we were no longer dead, empty vessels. Jesus came and filled us up inside and began to develop the family likeness in us. The Bible calls it 'sanctification'.

How can we recognize that the Holy Spirit is doing that in us? The same way we can recognize an apple tree – by looking at the fruit it is producing: 'the fruit of the Spirit is love' (Gal. 5:22). And that love proves to us that we are saved, according to 1 John 3:14. No love, no evidence of salvation.

That shouldn't be an uncomfortable thought. It should be an exciting beacon of light in a dark world. In the heart of the cycle of hatred and jealousy, it is compassion that can lift up those who are discouraged and depressed and restore hope to the hopeless. In the midst of the rush of selfishness and greed it is a love than can cross barriers that divide and break down walls of bitterness. It promises a church that is recognized not so much by the cross on its steeple as by the love in its congregation.

Genuine love

What will that love look like? We have already answered this question. The apostle John answers it too: '... let us not love with words or tongue but with actions and in truth'; 'If anyone has material possessions and sees his brother in need, but has no pity on him, how can the love of God be in him?' (1 John 3:18, 17).

Love is real only when it is given expression in acts of compassion, generosity and practical help. That is the family likeness, the way to identify a true Christian – one who loves, helps, comforts, encourages and gives. What a thought!

When William Booth of the Salvation Army died at the age of eighty-three on 20 August 1912, the message went out to Salvationists and to the world that 'the General has laid down his sword'. For fifty years he had worked tirelessly for the welfare and the rescue of the downtrodden, the poor and the needy, not only in London but also across the world, founding an Army that transformed the lives of millions.

In his final address three months earlier, to a congregation of seven thousand in London's Albert Hall, he had given this rousing testimony, even as his body was wearing out with age and exhaustion: 'While women weep as they do now, I'll fight; while little children go hungry as they do now, I'll fight; while men go to prison, in and out, in and out, I'll fight; while there yet remains one dark soul without the light of God, I'll fight – I'll fight to the very end!'[2]

It was the war-cry of an old warrior who had given himself without reserve for the kingdom of God. Forty thousand people attended his funeral at Olympia in west London. Salvation Army officers from all over the world 'knelt beside the casket to re-dedicate themselves to God and The Army. Along with them knelt thieves, tramps, harlots, the lost and outcast to whom Booth had given his heart.'[3]

Among many other tributes paid on that day was a moving comment from a converted prostitute, who had come to express her gratitude by placing three red carnations on the coffin of the one who had restored her to hope and dignity. By extraordinary chance she was seated next to royalty. Queen Mary, who had slipped into the funeral unannounced to pay her last respects, overheard that rescued prostitute whisper her greatest tribute: 'He cared for the likes of us.'[4]

Such is the family likeness and proof of a true follower of Christ – love that gives and gives and gives again.

3

The dignity of generosity

The church was born on the Day of Pentecost almost two thousand years ago. On that day, as recorded in the book of Acts, 120 apostles and disciples were gathered together in Jerusalem. One guess is that they were in the temple. No-one knows, but it was certainly in a fairly central and public place, where people could see what was going on. That made it so much more dramatic. Suddenly the wind howled around them (did they fear a hurricane?) and something that looked like flames of fire came and rested on the heads of every one of those disciples. 'All of them were filled with the Holy Spirit and began to speak in other tongues as the Spirit enabled them' (Acts 2:4).

That same day the community of the followers of Jesus began to grow, attracted by these sensational events and the public preaching of Peter. Three thousand people put their faith in Christ and were baptized. The disciples had become a growing community, and that demanded some sort of organization.

What sort of community?

The closest I have come to the fresh energy and vitality of the early church was my year and a half in Nepal in the 1970s. At that time the number of baptized believers in Nepal was still quite small, numbering only one or two thousand, and they were frequently harassed. Though evangelism was constitutionally illegal and could be punished by imprisonment, the church was active in outreach and sometimes paid the price. Baptisms took place in remote rivers in the mountains, far away from the eyes of potentially troublesome police. In spite of (maybe even because of) the hostility of the authorities, the church was beginning to grow rapidly.

We organized an evangelistic outreach in the mountains of eastern Nepal, and our teams, made up mostly of Nepali young men, scattered to village areas loaded with sacks of Gospels and Christian literature. To no-one's great surprise, one of the teams got into trouble. They had exhausted their literature supplies and had started the descent down the mountain back to the eastern town of Dharan. Word had travelled ahead of them, however, and the police were waiting for them as they walked into town. When we came to know about their predicament they were being held in the police station. Local Christians had rallied round and offered support, taking food to them and trying to intercede on their behalf.

I was back in Kathmandu when this happened, but as soon as I came to know about it I made the ten-hour journey back to Dharan, arriving late in the evening. It was dark when I knocked on the door of the believers' home where the rest of the team was staying. The house had no electric light and the team was gathered in a circle in the darkness, the small room lit only by one or two flickering candles that cast gaunt shadows on the walls. It was a simple home, built of wood with mud floors, little furniture and no luxuries. The believers were all on their knees, praying in hushed voices for the team members in trouble.

Pressure and difficulty bring out the best (and sometimes the worst) in everyone. What is inside us tends to come out when we are squeezed. When the world around proved hostile, what came out of these simple believers was sweet – a generosity of spirit that marked them out as different. They were driven to depend on one another as they struggled against the cultural tide.

I joined them in their prayer and stayed on with them for a few days until the members of our little group were released from custody with a warning. They weren't thrown to the lions or crucified – not even imprisoned, as so many Nepali Christians have been. Some people criticized us for running risks, but we gained an invaluable insight into the heartbeat of New Testament Christianity.

The early church must often have felt under pressure as a struggling minority community, driven together not just by a common cause against a hostile world but also by a deeply felt love for one another. We catch a glimpse of the church's priorities in Acts 2:42–47.

United around the truth

They 'devoted themselves to the apostles' teaching' (verse 42). We are deceived if we think that they had plenty of time to sit around listening to preachers and that is why they enjoyed going to meetings. Those folk were as busy as we are – not watching TV and playing video games perhaps, but earning their bread and keeping their difficult lives together. But in the midst of it all they loved to listen to the stories about Jesus and to learn from his teaching. There were plenty of people in the community who had heard Jesus in person and watched him as he touched the leprosy sufferers and healed the sick, and no doubt they gave first place to listening to what they remembered of his words. It was a question of priorities for them, as it is for us. They needed to know how to obey the will of Christ and to follow him in the midst of a hostile society. It was also a matter of survival. That is why they loved listening to preachers – not to sermon-taste, but to get their lives in line with the love of their hearts.

Committed to prayer

They were also enthusiastic about their commitment to 'fellow-ship, to the breaking of bread and to prayer' (verse 42). Perhaps they prayed a lot because they had a lot to pray about. If they hadn't stuck together in faith, they might have been torn apart. The prayer meeting was not a weekly duty or routine; they enjoyed the company of other believers and they instinctively turned to the one who held them together. It is of course true that they had no clocks – they just had time, and they used it to get together and bless one another. They took food in one another's company and celebrated the death of Jesus as they 'broke bread in their homes and ate together with glad and sincere hearts' (verse 46). And then they found comfort in sharing their needs and their fears with their heavenly Master.

Marked by generosity

'All the believers were together and had everything in common. Selling their possessions and goods, they gave to anyone as he had need' (verses 44–45). Step by step these verses take us closer to the secret of their enthusiasm for church and their love for one another. This was no formal religion devoted to church attend-ance and routine liturgy. It was a living and caring community of people who demonstrated their love for one another in practical ways. If someone was in need the other believers got together to raise the money – if necessary by selling their possessions – in order to meet that need. It was a community that knew how to give to one another. This kind of community can provide the support required for a radical and sacrificial lifestyle.

Here is the true meaning of 'fellowship': *koinōnia*, having all things in common. There is an essential sensitivity in *koinōnia*, sensing where the needs are and then practising a willingness to work together to meet those needs. It is much more than tea and biscuits after the service. This is true communion, what the church was meant to be from the beginning. Later we read: 'There were no needy persons among them. For from time to time those who owned lands or houses sold them, brought the money from the sales and put it at the apostles' feet, and it was distributed to anyone as he had need' (Acts 4:34–35).

This may seem a far cry from what we find in our churches today, but it is an ideal to aim at, not a slice of history to be admired. We have important lessons to take to heart, and examples to copy, from the early church. Is it any surprise that the result of this lifestyle was this: 'the Lord added to their number daily those who were being saved' (Acts 2:47)? And is it any surprise that the church in Nepal has been one of the fastest-growing Christian communities in all Asia in the past two or three decades?

The maturity of giving

A newborn baby is a picture of helplessness. No-one expects her to do much apart from making a loud noise when she is distressed and in need of help. She is a born receiver, and no-one criticizes her for expecting her benefactors to provide her with everything she needs – milk, clothing, care and attention. It is the divine plan for a baby to be totally on the receiving end for the first few years of life. A generous baby has yet to be born.

But as the little person begins to grow, she changes and develops. She learns to crawl around and experiment with the world, and in due time she discovers that she can feed herself, messily at first and then more skilfully. She begins to walk and then dress herself. She no longer needs to receive everything from Mum and Dad; she learns to be independent.

But there is a further stage the child must come to, in order to prove that she is growing up. She must begin to see that she is not alone in the world. There are others around to whom she must relate, some of whom need help. It is a further essential stage of growth when she discovers the need to be responsible to help others, to give to others, to feed and clothe those who are needier and weaker than herself. The person who always expects to receive from others and never learns to give is irresponsible, selfish and forever immature, and probably unpopular too. Giving to the needy, helping the weak, learning the simple art of generosity – these are signs of maturity. They are signs that someone has grown up and is ready to give birth to the next generation.

The same is true in the church and among believers.

When we were new Christians, spiritual babies just setting out on our spiritual journey, we needed all the help we could get. We needed to be fed the Word of God by grown-up Bible teachers. We needed to be instructed by our elders in the faith. Everything was a new discovery and we just drank it in. They were wonderful days, when all that was expected of us was to be looked after by others.

But as we grow up as Christians, things need to change. Tentatively at first, we begin to feed ourselves and to care for ourselves. Listening to the sermon each Sunday for our spiritual growth may still be helpful, but it should become less important than digging into the Word for ourselves in serious personal Bible study. If we have never discovered that spiritual food, we need to ask ourselves how much we have really grown.

But that is not the end of the story. Once we know how to feed ourselves with spiritual meat, it is time to look around and see who else also needs food.

Well do I remember my first faltering steps in preaching and witness. They were mostly unimpressive and unhelpful for those who heard them, but what progress for me! My first sermon was given to a small Brethren church in Switzerland, where I was spending a few months learning French in the Emmaus Bible School. A wonderful Austrian believer, Walter, was my mentor and encourager, and to my horror he arranged for me to preach one Sunday. I prepared my notes carefully and thoroughly and stumbled through a message on the resurrection, running out of material within ten minutes. I felt awful, and no-one complimented me, but what an important step it was for me! One small step for a baby Christian; one great leap towards maturity.

I am comforted by the thought that Billy Graham started out in a similar manner. Preaching to a small mountain congregation, his 'knees knocked and palms and brow were sticky. Billy began loud and fast. He had a bit of difficulty ... He ran out of words ... he ran out of thoughts ... but he got through all right.'[1] Billy Graham's first sermon lasted eight minutes. How poor the world would have been if he had never taken that step!

What we have applied to the spiritual realm is no less valid in the material. Christians need not only spiritual food; they need physical food too, and clothing and many other things. Baby Christians may feel it is as much as they can handle to look after their own needs, but as they grow up concern for others must grip their hearts. The time must come, if they are to grow, when they will look around and see who else needs help. Mature Christians should be able to look after more than the material needs of their own families and their own churches. They should also be able to watch out for those who are poorer and have greater material needs than themselves and give what they can to help them.

Paul exhorted the Philippian believers in these words: 'Each of you should look not only to your own interests, but also to the interests of others' (Phil. 2:4).

The dignity of giving

Generosity is not only a mark of maturity. It is also a sign of spiritual dignity. The church in Philippi stands out in the New Testament as a first-century model of generosity. The apostle Paul had a special affection for the Philippian Christians, as he had been personally blessed by their love. He used them as a role model when he wrote to the Corinthians, obviously trying to shame the church in Corinth into similar acts of generosity.

And now, brothers, we want you to know about the grace that God has given the Macedonian churches [one of which was Philippi]. Out of the most severe trial, their overflowing joy and their extreme poverty welled up in rich generosity. For I testify that they gave as much as they were able, and even beyond their ability. Entirely on their own, they urgently pleaded with us for the privilege of sharing in this service to the saints (2 Cor. 8:1–4).

Here is an example of Christians who had learned not only that giving was a mark of spiritual maturity, but also that there is dignity in helping others. They were no longer beggars asking for favours. They counted it a privilege and an honour to be able to help those in greater need; indeed, they 'pleaded' to be allowed to do so.

As sinners we are truly helpless people, dependent on the generosity of God. We are indeed beggars, and need to beg for his mercy and grace. But once we have been saved and lifted out of the gutter, as Paul said to the Corinthians, 'You will be made rich in every way so that you can be generous on every occasion, and through us your generosity will result in thanksgiving to God' (2 Cor. 9:11).

It is a shameful thing always to depend on other people's generosity. As Christians our first responsibility is to look to the needs of those who are less privileged and in greater need than ourselves. There is honour and dignity in generosity.

I recall meeting a beggar outside the railway station in Lucknow, north India. Like many beggars, his skin was ingrained with dirt, his clothes were ragged and torn and he had a long, unkempt beard, probably crawling with lice. I cannot recall how I discovered that he spoke perfect English, but I was intrigued and squatted down beside him on the dusty steps. I asked him for his story.

'I was a college lecturer in Calcutta,' he told me. 'I lived with my family, had a good job and was earning enough money.'

'But why, then, are you here in Lucknow, begging in the street?'

He gave a haunting reply. 'I was bored with life, and I discovered that I can earn more money begging for three hours a day than I could earn as a teacher in Calcutta. I work shorter hours, it is easier, there is no responsibility and I earn more money. That is why I am a beggar.'

I do not know the full story of this pathetic figure. Maybe his family had thrown him out; maybe he had had a mental breakdown; maybe he was a drug addict or an alcoholic. But I do know that, as a beggar, he had no sense of dignity, no self-respect in the best sense of the term. His life values had become hideously distorted.

My mind goes back to the old man who lived in Bilgram, surrounded by his family and a few chickens. What dignity there was in that man! Not the dignity of high birth or cash in the bank, but the dignity of knowing that he was the master of his small world and that he had no need to be ashamed of his lot in life.

4

Lifestyle choices

'What are your ambitions in life? What do you want to be?'

When I was still squeaky-voiced and wearing shorts I dreamed of what I would become in life. My ideals usually revolved around being an engine driver or an airline pilot. Those were the glamorous days of steam, when it was still fun to take a train and few people were concerned if it didn't arrive on time. The thrill was in the journey. Our home was above a railway tunnel and we used to watch and wait for the engines to emerge from its mouth, belching smoke. Our young world was entranced by the steaming monsters that made our house rattle. The story was told that just after the Great War the tunnel beneath our foundations had caved in and the stables had disappeared into the hole. One of the carriage horses was killed. Such was the glamour of the steam age on the railways.

But things change fast with the generations and today you will get a very different answer. 'I want to be a movie star ... a pop singer ... a footballer. I am going to be rich and famous!' Fashions and fads have moved on. The glamour of the steam age and the early thrill of air travel have given way to the media and the magnetic appeal of riches and fame.

The gift of freedom

One of the more extraordinary of God's gifts to us is the freedom to decide what we want to be – the freedom to make those choices, the freedom to decide what we want to make of our lives. The modern world has made 'choice' one of its golden watchwords. It was not always like that, but our western world offers great opportunities, with worldwide travel, higher education, exercise and entertainment all available to the vast majority. It all sounds so good, if only people knew how to make good choices and enjoy true freedom. Sadly, most people are better equipped to make bad choices.

Jimmy (not his real name) was a close friend who was having difficulties in his marriage. We knew each other well and he asked for my advice. Jimmy was a Christian. He had worked for a period in full-time ministry and was active in his home church. He knew the Bible well enough to know what he ought to do. We went for a long drive in the countryside and then climbed a hill together and sat on the grass overlooking his home town.

It is not hard to give advice when the issues are so black and white. In this case, he had become bored with the routines of family life and had had a fling with an attractive woman, who made him feel young again. I listened at length to his sorry tale and together we looked at the options ahead of him.

On the one hand were his faithful wife and two young daughters, whom he adored. The last thing he wanted was to hurt them. Then there was his reputation in the church and Christian community, his service for God and his future. On the other hand was his attraction to the young woman who had, for the moment, made him feel so good about himself. She also was married. If he pursued this relationship, it would cost him his loving family, his future ministry, his reputation and some of his friends – everything that, to that point, he had held dear – not to mention the damage it would do to his relationship with God. It would also devastate the family of the woman he was drawn to.

'Jimmy,' I said, 'it seems very clear what you need to do. It might cost you some pain and be very hard to do. You might feel you have lost something exciting. But the alternative is too tragic to contemplate. Now you have to choose.'

We prayed together.

I left him, knowing exactly what he was going to do. In the face of all the evidence that made logical good sense he was going to make the wrong choice. That is just what he did. Turning his back on his wife and causing endless pain to her and to his young children, he went through the agony of divorce, left his church and his secure circle of friends and followed the tug of his emotions. By every standard Jimmy made a bad choice.

Why is it that we so often make bad choices, when Christ has set us free to make good choices?

Such is the stuff of everyday life. Most of the choices we face are trivial. Nescafé or Maxwell House? Gap or Levi? Which one of eighty brands of shampoo or a hundred types of cheese should we buy? Some choices, however, such as that facing Jimmy, are far from trivial and have far-reaching consequences. To abort or not to abort? To cheat on my spouse or to remain faithful? To chase my great ambition or to be passionate about the will of God? To indulge in an orgy of selfishness or to give God the credit of knowing what is best for my future welfare and happiness?

Many years ago our ancestor Eve was faced with a decision of life-sized magnitude in the Garden of Eden (Gen. 3:1–4). The serpent had given her a choice: to eat the fruit or not to eat? It seemed like a trivial matter of little consequence. God had given her total freedom in her lifestyle, except for this one thing: 'You must not eat fruit from the tree that is in the middle of the garden.' That was one choice with momentous consequences. Should she listen to the slimy reptile or believe the word of her great benefactor?

And the serpent told her, 'when you eat of it your eyes will be opened'. It seemed such a small decision to make and the rewards appeared very enticing. What should she do? She had to choose.

It is wrong to try to pass the buck when faced with such decisions. Owning up and taking responsibility do not come naturally to any of us. We are responsible for being the kind of people we are, just as Eve and her husband Adam had to take responsibility for opening the door to evil that has wrecked the world. Small choice; big responsibility; no excuse.

In this chapter and the next we shall look at some of the choices we have to make in our relationship to our world. They might sometimes seem trivial and of little consequence. But they could make the difference between life and death in our own lives and the lives of many others. Adam and Eve made lifestyle choices that affected the whole of human history. It may not always be easy, but how important it is that we learn to get it right!

Who will be number one?

Not long after Adam and Eve made their big mistake in the Garden of Eden their son Cain made one of his big life choices. What a mistake that was, too! Cain carelessly offered some of his harvest to God, and his deep-rooted selfishness resulted in bitter jealousy of his brother Abel when God rejected his offering in favour of Abel's animal sacrifice. Jealousy is a great evil and it still destroys many people. Cain was so inwardly eaten up by jealousy that he caught his brother in the field and murdered him (Gen. 4:2b–9).

Why was Cain so stupid and small-minded?

The problem was in his attitude, and his attitude led to some bad choices. Unwilling to give away his best possessions, he offered the bare minimum to God. What a contrast to his brother Abel, whose big-hearted generosity gave God the best he had to offer! Cain got what was coming to him. God rejected his measly token, which awakened his jealousy and led to his murderous outburst of anger.

'Where is your brother Abel?' God asked.

'I don't know,' Cain replied. 'Am I my brother's keeper?'

Yes, of course you are, Cain. You are responsible and have to pay the price of your bad decision. It is a mark of selfishness in the heart that says, 'I am not responsible for my brother's welfare.' Jesus said, 'Love one another', because as his disciples we are responsible for one another.

Cain was simply stating the old philosophy, 'I am number one, and other people are not my problem.' Who is in charge? Cain said, 'I am.'

Cain's kind of selfishness and greed became all too common in the hearts of people from that point on throughout the Bible story. Esau, son of Isaac, was no better (Gen. 2:29–34). He was in the field and he was hungry. Jacob, his brother, was boiling lentil stew, and Esau demanded some of it: 'let me have some of that red stew! I'm famished!'

Jacob, however, was smart and schemed to cheat his brother of the blessing of his birthright. 'First sell me your birthright,' he said.

So, for a stomachful of food, Esau threw away the blessing of his birthright. What a picture of thoughtless greed! A short-term gain at the price of long-term blessing.

Are we any different? 'Give me what I want. Give it to me now,' we tritely say, indifferent to the needs of others, forgetful of the blessing we throw away in our desire to have what we want, and to have it now. Give it to whom? 'Give it to me.'

Get and grab

One of my simple pleasures in life is to go to charity jumble sales. It is still possible to find one somewhere in the neighbourhood most Saturdays, raising funds for the Boy Scouts or Cats Protection, or some other worthy cause. They serve the community by helping people to dispose of their unwanted things with a good conscience and by recycling junk that seems too good to take to the dump. With a sharp eye you can find a bargain for a few pennies.

Jumble sales are not only places to find a bargain; they also afford a wonderful opportunity to observe a social tradition. Half an hour before the doors open a line begins to form. People wait patiently, some clinging to large, empty, cloth or plastic bags. But they do not usually talk to one another. There is a certain intensity in their eyes, which precludes social chatter, and it increases as the time approaches for the doors to open. When that moment finally arrives, the first through the doors are in a hurry, making a beeline for the bargains, determined to get ahead of anyone else who might have an eye on the same prize. There is a certain amount of pushing and shoving.

It is a fine opportunity to observe the 'get and grab' ambition that lies in the hearts of most of us. You will find the same intensity in the sale queues that form outside large stores after Christmas. It is competitive, ruthless and definitely 'me first'. Jumble-sale greed breaks no rules, but it exposes an ugly streak in us all.

The tenth commandment stands to judge us every time we want to grab something that belongs to, or is needed by, someone else. This is a truly twenty-first-century, capitalist-mentality sin.

'You shall not covet your neighbour's house.

You shall not covet your neighbour's wife, or his manservant or maidservant, his ox or donkey, or anything that belongs to your neighbour' (Exod. 20:17).

The apostle Paul said that covetousness and greed are as evil as immorality: 'among you there must not be even a hint of sexual immorality, or of any kind of impurity, or of greed, because these are improper for God's holy people' (Eph. 5:3). It is not a small sin to want to keep up with the Joneses.

James says that covetousness is the most subtle and dangerous of all sins, because it leads on to much more serious and harmful evil. 'What causes fights and quarrels among you? Don't they come from your desires that battle within you? You want something but don't get it. You kill and covet, but you cannot have what you want' (James 4:1–2).

In my early years working with a team of evangelists in India, one annual highlight always caused a stir. Each year around November a convoy of vans arrived, bringing new team members from Europe to work with us. They had driven the seven thousand miles, which used to be the easy and cheap way to get to India.

They also brought huge quantities of supplies with them – items unavailable in India or useful to our mission. There was always a large quantity of second-hand clothing, and our team members had the privilege of choosing items that might be useful for their wardrobe. And this is what opened my eyes to how truly spiritual some of us really were.

The competitive urge suddenly awoke in the most godly among us – the desire to grab and take the best before anyone else could get it, and the anger and jealousy that came to life when someone got an item someone else was keen to have. I remember watching my team leader fighting over a pair of jeans that someone else also wanted. It was an extraordinarily ugly display of greed. And I am ashamed to say that I found the same urges in me. Beware that inner serpent!

It comes into our living-rooms in the form of the ads on TV. The media manipulators know what stirs us to want what we don't need. How can we be satisfied with a Ford when our neighbour has a BMW? How can we contemplate a holiday in Cornwall when our workmate is flying to the Caribbean? It is all calculated to make us want more than we need, and sometimes more than we can afford – an evil close to the heart of our prosperous society. 'I want it, and I will have it!' It may be a small desire but it can, and sometimes does, lead to murder and war. These are bad choices.

No-one can legislate for how we should live, and we must all decide on a lifestyle suitable to our position in life. No two people will make the same decision on that, and we must beware of being judgmental about other people's life decisions. But one thing is true of us all: we have a clear command to avoid envy and greed.

The generous lifestyle

You sometimes won't recognize them when you meet them. They don't look especially pious or holy, and sometimes they even live well. They don't necessarily drive a broken-down, second-hand car. Sometimes they drive a Jaguar and sometimes they ride a bicycle.

John Sharritt was a very wealthy man when I first met him in Calcutta many years ago. In fact, that is why we met – he had a lot of money and was looking for ways to spend it before he died. He saw no purpose in depriving himself of blessing and leaving all his wealth behind to people who might not spend it as well as he. So he set out to look for good causes in which he could invest. We were one of them. His great passion was to give people the Word of God, and he had decided that those in his home country (the United States) already had adequate access to the gospel and he should look elsewhere. He came to India.

Strictly speaking, he planned to give his money not to us but to anyone who would print or buy Gospels and then distribute them to people who could read them, in the hope that they would turn to Christ to be saved. Over the next several years we received tens of thousands of dollars, with which we purchased subsidized Gospels to be distributed in our street evangelism. When, finally, John died, he surely went to a rich reward in heaven. He had made a significant lifestyle choice and invested well, using his latter years to give away the surplus with which God had endowed him.

But those who have chosen the generous lifestyle are not always wealthy. In fact, the opposite is probably more often true. I think of Jim, an elderly supporter and prayer partner of our work in Pakistan, who lives in Ireland. Jim wrote to me, 'I sent no money for a long time, as I have very little. I sent on £1,500 years ago for the children of India. I have given 40% of my money to the Lord's work over the years ... I think I did my bit moneywise ...' God treasures the big-heartedness of those who have relatively little and have chosen the generous lifestyle.

We can probably all think of people who are always looking for ways of giving – not only their money, but hospitality, help and service. It is a lifestyle choice made by those whose lives have been enriched by the grace of God. And of all lifestyles to choose, it is surely the most blessed.

Let us make our decisions and make them well. Honour the Lord, avoid covetousness and love one another.

5

Focus and ambition

Government economic policy involves deciding whether to encourage saving or to encourage spending. For some people the highlight of each month is the day when the Bank of England decides whether to raise or lower interest rates. That 0.25% decision affects the mortgage rate, the share index, the rate of inflation and the cost of living, the mood of the market and the mood of the country. For others it is the daily stock-market report, the FTSE or Wall Street index that tells whether their wealth has grown or shrunk.

People hang on the outcome of these decisions as though they were life or death. Fortunes were lost when the dot.com bubble burst in 2000, and those who had expected a bonanza when they bought their lastminute.com shares found them plummeting. Big business scandals shake people not so much by the evil they reveal in society as by the damage they do to personal fortunes. It has become a national disease; we accumulate wealth while a third of the world starves.

The secret of contentment

Statistics tell us that 28% of UK households have no savings and 21% have less than £1,500.[1] But go into the High Street on a Saturday afternoon and you will see where the hoarding instinct is driving people – accumulating toys for a rainy day rather than cash. Or if not toys, clothes, many of which will hang or lie unused once the winds of fashion begin to blow in another direction. In our society people tend to estimate their value by the possessions they have collected, the label on their shirt or jeans, and the model of the car outside the front door.

What a far cry from the secret of contentment outlined by Jesus for his disciples in the Sermon on the Mount!

> 'Therefore I tell you, do not worry about your life, what you will eat or drink; or about your body, what you will wear. Is not life more important than food, and the body more important than clothes? ... seek first his kingdom and his righteousness, and all these things will be given to you as well' (Matt. 6:25, 33).

Peace of mind is not an insurance policy or a five-year warranty on the gadgetry in our homes. It is an attitude. The apostle Paul had learned it well:

> I have learned to be content whatever the circumstances. I know what it is to be in need, and I know what it is to have plenty. I have learned the secret of being content in any and every situation, whether well fed or hungry, whether living in plenty or in want (Phil. 4:11–12).

It is a decision we all have to make: where should we store our possessions? Jesus told us not to accumulate surplus treasures on earth, for 'where your treasure is, there your heart will be also', and accumulated treasure becomes what the Bible calls idolatry. 'No-one can serve two masters ... You cannot serve both God and Money' (Matt. 6:19–24).

Some have concluded that Jesus glorified poverty or exhorted his followers to a kind of ascetic, hippy lifestyle, and the monastic movement with its emphasis on poverty is testimony to that conviction. Indeed, didn't Jesus say, 'Blessed are you who are poor, for yours is the kingdom of God' (Luke 6:20)?

I sometimes find myself driving behind a beaten-up old jalopy, rust spots staining its battered wings, its paintwork patchy and proudly grimy. I cringe when I see the fish sticker on the back window, proclaiming that it is owned by a Christian. It is testimony to the mentality that poverty, scruffiness and disreputability are a proud statement of anti-materialism – a strange way of proclaiming, 'We are Christians; we are different; the world is not our home!'

John Wesley gave some sane advice to his followers, many of whom were very ordinary people who lived on the borderlines of poverty. His counsel is both wise and witty.

> Do not stink above ground. This is a bad fruit of laziness; use all diligence to be clean … Whatever clothes you have, let them be whole; no rents, no tatters, no rags. These are a scandal to either man or woman, being another fruit of vile laziness. Mend clothes, or I shall never expect you to mend your lives. Let none ever see a ragged Methodist.[2]

No less than flashy exhibitionism, glorying in poverty fails to honour the Lord. It is an extreme, the opposite extreme to materialism – though definitely preferable to the arrogance that proclaims, 'We can afford the best. We not only kept up with the neighbours; we overtook them!' Jesus never glorified poverty or held it up as an ideal for his followers. If he promised a blessing to the poor, it was because of his concern to lift up the downtrodden and to appeal to the underprivileged, and in no way to promote poverty. Material deprivation is as evil as materialistic idolatry.

On the contrary, the Scriptures are clear about the wisdom of making allowance for our future and providing responsibly for family needs. 'If anyone does not provide for his relatives, and especially for his immediate family,' says Paul, 'he has denied the faith' (1 Tim. 5:8). Strong words, and a powerful warning to act responsibly.

Here are more wise words:

> Go to the ant, you sluggard;
>   consider its ways and be wise!
> ... it stores its provisions in summer
>   and gathers its food at harvest.

There are about eight thousand species of ant in the world, and they are all social insects that live their lives in communities, normally known as colonies. There is no such thing as a selfish or lonely ant. At the heart of the colony is the queen, whose whole adult life is given to producing the next generation and to being served by the next rank in the strict caste system, the males. The vast mass of the colony are the workers, whose lives are dedicated to service and industry – building the nest, protecting it from enemies and providing food in every season. Study the ant, said wise Solomon, and learn the lessons of selfless hard work in providing for the needs of others.

Foolish are those who rest their hopes in the accumulation of costly toys and games for a rainy day. 'Command those who are rich in this present world not to be arrogant nor to put their hope in wealth, which is so uncertain, but to put their hope in God, who richly provides us with everything for our enjoyment' (1 Tim. 6:17).

Chasing the golden egg

Nowadays the acquisition of things has become so acceptable that most people consider material prosperity to be a human right. Mass advertising, internet and TV shopping, the boom mentality of the great shopping malls – these are the worship centres of our day. Our capitalist economy requires people to buy what they do not need in order to fuel the nation's prosperity. It is no surprise that the pursuit of wealth has become many people's highest goal.

Jesus told the story of a farmer who went out to sow his seed (Luke 8:4–15). He scattered the seed far and wide and it fell on different kinds of ground. Some of the seed fell on the path and was eaten up by the birds. Some fell on the rock and could find no soil for its roots, so it withered and died. Other seed fell among thorns, which grew along with the wheat and destroyed it. 'This is the meaning of the parable,' said Jesus. 'The seed that fell among thorns stands for those who hear, but as they go on their way they are choked by life's worries, riches and pleasures, and they do not mature.'

This is the bad choice that has destroyed the life of many zealous Christians. Note again that the Bible nowhere teaches that poverty is a virtue. Jesus taught that, as human beings, we have inalienable rights to food and clothing – the essentials of a reasonable standard of living: 'your heavenly Father knows that you need them' (Matt. 6:32).

Note also that, in the Scriptures, mainly in the Old Testament, wealth is viewed as a mark of God's blessing. 'Remember the LORD your God,' said Moses, 'for it is he who gives you the ability to produce wealth' (Deut. 8:18). It was a mark of God's blessing that he gave Solomon 'wealth, riches and honour, such as no king who was before you ever had and none after you will have' (2 Chron. 1:12).

Jesus stayed happily in the homes of wealthy people (Luke 19:5), accepted anointing with an expensive perfume in Bethany (John 12:3), and was buried in the tomb of a wealthy admirer (Matt. 27.57), who was also a disciple.

It is never the *possession* of riches that is criticized in Scripture, but our *attitude* to riches, which can become so destructive. Wealth is condemned whenever it is loved, idolized and used illegitimately. The ambition to be rich and the passion to possess are curses that have destroyed the faith of many. The pursuit of wealth as an all-consuming ambition is idolatry. It is a bad lifestyle choice.

In the week in which I am writing this, the newspapers have been focusing on the arrogance of a self-made multi-millionaire, Nicholas van Hoogstraten, who faces ten years in jail for his alleged part in the killing of a business rival.[3] Mr van Hoogstraten appears to have been a man of much flair and many follies. Having accumulated a fortune in ruthless property-dealing, he set out to build himself a lasting memorial – a £30-million home to be named Hamilton Palace, the largest private dwelling to be built in Britain in the twentieth century.

The palace, set in the gently rolling East Sussex countryside, has a frontage wider than that of Buckingham Palace. It should have been completed in 2000. Due to a dispute with the builders, however, construction stopped and the half-built structure now stands incomplete and forlorn, guarded by Rottweilers and 2.5-m barbed-wire fences. 'Planks of wood, concrete blocks and a discarded pair of Wellington boots lie beside the unrendered walls that were intended, by now, to be used to hang van Hoogstraten's Holbein, two Turners and other paintings.'[4] The unfinished roofs are leaking and nature is slowly reducing this relic of human pride to a ruin.

Not only was van Hoogstraten's dream palace intended to house his personal fortune, but 'there, he said, his body would repose pharaoh-like in a chamber which would last for thousands of years'.[5] What a monument to human vanity! And yet it should stand as a symbol of the multitude of minor follies we all too easily submit to – our own small mausoleums, which we are tempted to construct for our own pleasure and glory. We should beware the tendency to judge Mr van Hoogstraten before looking inside our own tempted egos. That too is a lifestyle choice.

'People who want to get rich fall into temptation and a trap and into many foolish and harmful desires that plunge men into ruin and destruction,' warns Paul. 'For the love of money is a root of all kinds of evil' (1 Tim. 6:9–10). The Bible has many such warnings.

Life in the deep end

Debt is another, all-too-common aspect of our modern way of life. A recent newspaper article stated that Britons have an accumulated debt of £800 billion; we are the biggest debtors in all Europe: 'On average, those with mortgages now have total loans of nearly £63,000 each, including £1,500 on credit cards and store cards and £3,000 of other loans.'[6]

The BBC website ran a headline, 'Britons in debt spiral'[7] which underscored the seriousness of the debt plague in modern society. They reported on a survey of 8,000 debt case studies, conducted by the Citizens Advice Bureau, which revealed that 'total debt as a percentage of average annual income has increased from 54% in 1993 to 70% in 2002.'

Living in debt is a totally acceptable and normal part of twenty-first-century life. It is a convenience that keeps the economy going and provides access to much-needed lump sums of cash for both necessary and desirable purchases. Few students would get through their education without taking a Government loan. There is a Bible verse that says, 'Owe no man anything' (Rom. 13:8, Authorized Version), but that does not mean we should not own a credit card or have a mortgage.

Nevertheless, whole books have been written warning of the dangers of losing control of debt convenience – allowing a facility that can help us manage our budgets to become a monster that controls our lives. Like the furry tiger kitten that looks so soft and playful, it doesn't always remain so innocent. The tiger cub grows up, sharpens its claws and threatens to tear you apart unless you keep it under control. The Bible (as well as today's newspaper) gives some clear warnings concerning debt. As a short-term means of meeting needs, debt is permissible and acceptable to

God; but when debt grows to dominate our lifestyle it is not only unacceptable but a curse.

The BBC web page invited readers to respond to their news of the debt spiral. Here is a summary of the comments from seventy-six people who wrote in:

- The largest number, almost half, in some way blamed the ease with which credit can be obtained, accusing credit-card companies of irresponsibility.
- Several identified student loans and house prices as the culprit in forcing people into debt to survive the rat-race.
- There were a number of comments along the lines that 'the Government must take responsibility for controlling this'.
- About fifteen people recognized that ultimately greed is the problem. No-one is to blame but the debtor, unable to say 'No' to a culture that encourages greed:
  'Don't get sucked into the "must-have", "coolest-thing-to-have" trend.'
  'This situation is merely a symptom of people's short-termist "must-have-now" mentality.'
  'Most people blame costly education, or tempting credit-card offers and various other things, for their debts. But they never blame themselves!'
  'It's greed, and the only irresponsible ones are the borrowers who can't wait for a few months to have that holiday, that new car or that stylish new mobile phone ...'
  'It's simple: if you can't afford it, don't buy it.'

The alarming thing is that our culture, and our lifestyle decisions, have brought us as a society to the point of assuming that we can continue indefinitely to live beyond our means – that if we cannot swim it is acceptable just to keep our heads above water. When twenty-five million British households have 'total borrowings of seven times their quarterly disposable income',[8] have we gone too far? Should Christians live in permanent debt?

The BBC web page reported that 'one-quarter of those surveyed were receiving treatment for stress, depression and anxiety, with money worries making matters worse in most cases'. There must be a better way to live.

Godly advice

God gave the Jews a marvellous way of keeping their debts under control. 'At the end of every seven years you must cancel debts.' And then he told them how to do it – very practical, very detailed. 'Every creditor shall cancel the loan he has made to his fellow Israelite. He shall not require payment from his fellow Israelite or brother' (Deut. 15:1–2).

Can you imagine how Barclays or Natwest would handle that?

I was once refused a credit card by one of the major banks. I was somewhat offended. I took it as their way of saying that I was a poor risk, probably unreliable and unable to repay. I wrote and complained about the slur on my integrity. A polite reply assured me that no such insult was implied, but I was still not welcome to join them. In reality, I was probably refused because my income was less than their rules permitted. Perhaps I should have quoted Deuteronomy: '… do not be hard-hearted or tight-fisted towards your poor brother. Rather be open-handed and freely lend him whatever he needs.' God was one step ahead of the greedy money-lenders: 'Be careful not to harbour this wicked thought: "The seventh year, the year for cancelling debts, is near," so that you do not show ill will towards your needy brother and give him nothing' (Deut. 15:7–9).

I don't think the bank would have been impressed by that argument. The point is not that God was laying down laws for money-lenders for all time, but he was teaching a very valid and important lesson. It's all right to lend and it's all right to borrow, but remember:

- The lender should be generous and big-hearted towards the poor and the needy.
- The borrower should not stay in debt a day longer than necessary.

The laws God was giving were applied to his family, the Israelites. They did not apply outside the family (see Deut. 15:3). God was giving important lessons for his own people – generosity in the heart of the benefactors, responsibility in the heart of the indebted. He was not laying down principles for an international economy.

If we have run up a debt, it is our Christian responsibility to count debt repayment responsibly – to keep our spending under control, lest it strangle and overwhelm us, and to live modestly within our means. That is a lifestyle choice that only we can make for ourselves.

There is a further problem here, which is even more serious. Some people become compulsive shoppers and sink into debt because they feel the acquisition of things is essential to their security and a sense of worth. Those who feel unworthy unless they keep spending on luxuries they cannot afford need urgent help. Shopaholics suffer from a recognized addiction, akin to kleptomania, for which appropriate counselling is available. The urge to spend and to buy relates to the need for a sense of significance. There is a solution to the problem, not least in the significance Christ provides through the gospel.

Those who have borrowed money and promised to return it need to make it a high priority to keep their word. No-one living in debt should spend money on other luxuries until that debt is cleared. That is a matter of essential Christian integrity and honesty, and is not to be taken lightly.

'Let no debt remain outstanding,' said the apostle Paul, 'except the continuing debt to love one another' (Rom. 13:8). Living free from the curse of long-term indebtedness is a lifestyle choice.

Spiritual materialism

Before we move on, we should look briefly at just one of the more unusual choices before us in the Christian world: the choice of spiritual materialism. That should be a contradiction in terms.

On the back of a prosperous world has come the subtle doctrine that it is possible to have our cake and eat it. An enthusiastic Christian movement has sprung up that teaches that God actually planned that we should be materially rich as a sign of his spiritual blessing. Now that is a lifestyle choice that anyone can accept with ease! But is it true?

To give a taste of this doctrine, let me quote from one of its foremost advocates. This comes from the lead article in a recent magazine:

> One afternoon in 1998, the voice of the Lord came to me as I sat in my office, praying in the Spirit … I heard Him say:
>
> *I want you to buy a brand new airplane – right now.*
>
> His words surprised me. To begin with, I didn't think I needed a new airplane. I liked the one I already had …
>
> When I asked the Lord why He wanted me to buy a new one, He said, *I'm tired of this old airplane, old house, old car, old clothes mentality among My people.*[9]

How can the writer justify this passion for prosperity? Look at this fascinating biblical justification. It comes from the story of Jesus riding into Jerusalem on the back of a donkey.

> Notice that this was not some worn-out, old, swayback donkey that no one wanted. No, Jesus specifically said it was one that had never been used. That's what He needed – a 'new' donkey, not a used one.[10]

This is not the place for a full investigation of this unusual doctrine, except to warn that all that glitters is not gold. But increasing numbers of well-meaning, enthusiastic Christians are being drawn into something that looks both biblically acceptable and seductively attractive. Of course, anyone would be a fool who would not be tempted by the possibility of a private aeroplane, first-class travel and expensive designer clothes, not to mention perfect health, if it were legitimately available.

The advocates of the 'health and wealth gospel' are quite right in saying that God wants the very best for his children. They rightly criticize the gloom-and-doom message that often passes for orthodox Christian doctrine. But they have made a tragic mistake in their understanding of the legitimacy and availability of this golden ideal.

Not least among the evils of this teaching is its obscene indifference to a world where so many millions live in abject poverty while certain so-called men and women of faith enjoy material luxuries, which they claim are their right as Christians. But the main thing they have got wrong is the timing of this blessing. There is indeed a day coming when there will be no more tears, 'no more death or mourning or crying or pain'. One day God will step in and say: 'I am making everything new!' and we shall enter a city of gold and precious stones (Rev. 21:4–5, 11–21). But we have got to wait a while before we get there. It will happen only when all the other wrongs and injustices in society are righted at the great Judgment Day.

Those who hope for material prosperity and perfect health, 'named and claimed' and magically dropped from heaven in the here and now, are destined to a life of frustration and disappointment, if not disillusionment and anger. Beware those who make unfounded promises and invite us to dream impossible dreams!

Taking responsibility

God has made us creatures of decision, with the power to choose and direct how we live. What an opportunity that gives us!

It is, sadly, escapist to pretend that we are just the products of our environment, though there is obviously some truth in that belief. Someone must have believed it in a recent case before the courts in America. On trial was an FBI agent accused of embezzling and gambling away $2,000 of FBI money. His defence? He argued that his gambling behaviour was a handicap, protected under the 'Americans with Disabilities' Act.[11] Incredibly, the court acquitted him.

In reality, the story highlights the sad life of someone who got into the habit of making bad choices and then tried to evade responsibility for the consequences. It is evidence of a pathetic human weakness and inability to make good choices or fashion a decent lifestyle. It further illustrates the fallenness of humankind (for which we must each ultimately take full responsibility) and our inability to pull ourselves up by our bootstraps.

By the grace of God, however – and this is the gospel – we have the power through Christ and his indwelling Holy Spirit to make those choices in life that mould us into Christ's image – which implies deliberately turning our back on bad lifestyle choices. In the next chapter we investigate some of the exciting alternatives open to us.

6

Extra-mile living

By any standards Robert Arthington was an eccentric. But he was also a very shrewd businessman, who invested his inherited riches so well that he accumulated a large fortune. What he is remembered for, however, is the passion of his life that marked him out in his day as a man of extraordinary generosity who poured untold wealth into the work of the gospel and the needs of the poor.

'Arthington's millions'

That is not how he started out in life. Robert was born in Leeds in the north of England on 20 May 1823. His parents were committed Christians and leading figures in the Society of Friends (the Quakers) and his father was a businessman and owned a brewery. He used to provide a barrel of ale for the annual meeting of the Leeds Quakers, until a crisis of conscience forced him to close up the business in 1846 and become a strong advocate of the temperance movement.

Because he was born into wealth, the young Robert did not

need to work. Instead, after concluding his studies at Cambridge, he developed a wide variety of other interests and hobbies. He was an amateur musician and composer. He wrote articles on *The Fertilisation of the Soil*, *Preventable Accidents* and *The Maintenance of Health*. Above all, he was a collector and a hoarder, 'a congenital magpie as well as a bounding dilettante'.[1] He collected seashells and became an authority on coins. His family home was more like a museum than a residence, containing, 'among other things, the most comprehensive collection of umbrellas and spectacles in the land'.[2]

But, as a follower of Christ, he made some other significant life-style choices, and it is for these that he is best remembered. When his father died, Robert inherited £200,000, a fortune by the standards of the day.[3] He began to make wise investments, notably in British and American railways, which increased his wealth still further. But money did not go to his head. Quite the opposite. He became known in his neighbourhood as the 'Miser of Headingley' (a district of Leeds) for the extreme simplicity of his lifestyle. The passion that began to consume him was the promotion of Christian missions overseas and the advance of the gospel, especially but not exclusively in Africa.

With great secrecy he began to give away large sums of money to needy mission societies. He supported the new Church Missionary Society outreach to Uganda; he provided the Baptists with a steamer for use on the Congo River, and the London Missionary Society with another for work on Lake Tanganyika. He wanted to help form a chain of mission stations to constitute 'a line of gospel light across the "dark continent".' He started his own mission in northeast India.

Towards the end of his life, he discovered that he had miscalculated his fortune; his investments were earning him much more than he realized. He immediately sent off £10,000 for the relief of those suffering from famine in India. And when he finally died in 1900, he still left behind almost £1 million. His will distributed nine-tenths of his fortune to missions, with the special request that some be used to give every language group copies of the Gospels of Luke and John and the Acts of the Apostles in the vernacular. The Arthington Trust continued to donate generously to the work of missions until 1936.

£1 million no longer sounds so much in this day of lottery draws, but a hundred years ago it was a huge sum. 'Arthington's Millions' have earned their place in the history of missions, quite apart from the incalculable good they have done across the world. But the example of big-hearted Robert Arthington is happily not unique. Generosity in different forms has characterized the people of God throughout the centuries, and Arthington was by no means the first or the last to make it a personal passion and life ambition. He is not a hero to be admired from a distance, but a model to inspire us to imitation, an illustration of what it means to live beyond the call of duty. Such big-heartedness is at the root of much of Jesus' teaching for disciples.

Extra-mile mentality

Jesus' most famous sermon contains many teachings that have been both widely admired and largely ignored. Some have given the Sermon on the Mount the status of admirable but utterly unreal idealism, skirting round its message as though it were designed only for the exceptional saint and not for every disciple.

Among its more embarrassing paragraphs is the one where Jesus begins, 'You have heard that it was said, "Eye for eye, and tooth for tooth." But I tell you, Do not resist an evil person' (Matt. 5:38–39).

'Hang on!' we interrupt. 'Do you mean to say I should turn my back on justice and allow thieves to rob me, and wickedness to flourish? Turning the other cheek and going the extra mile is no longer reasonable. Underdogs need to stand up for their rights or be trampled on.' Or, as Martin Luther expressed it in his inimitable prose, was Jesus mistakenly applauding 'the crazy saint who let the lice nibble at him and refused to kill any of them on account of this text, maintaining that he had to suffer and could not resist evil'?[4] Great teaching for the Middle Ages, but bypassed in our modern age by social pressure and survival requirements.

No, Jesus was not giving permission for unscrupulous tyrants, thieves and corrupt officials to take advantage of us. He was illustrating what it means to live to the full as his disciples, to live beyond the call of duty, to be big-hearted and generous in our attitude to life. He emphasized his point four times:

- 'If someone strikes you …'
- 'If someone wants to sue you …'
- 'If someone forces you to go one mile …'
- If someone 'asks you, and … wants to borrow from you …' (Matt. 5:39–42)

What choices are open to us?

'If someone strikes you …'

'If someone strikes you on the right cheek, turn to him the other also.'

Revenge is a fundamental, knee-jerk instinct, but it is also a choice. It is sometimes called self-defence or even justice, but the essential animal instinct is for revenge – eye for eye, tooth for tooth, or worse if possible. The natural reaction in all of us is the snake instinct: strike back if someone treads on your tail. The mind naturally turns to the dramatic and the violent – the murder of Leon Trotsky in Mexico City with an ice-pick in 1940, hunted down over a decades by a vengeful Stalin, or the execution of Nicolae Ceausescu of Romania on Christmas Day 1989 by citizens seeking revenge for his years of tyranny.

But we need to bring our insights closer to home. Consider a recent newspaper headline: 'Pensioner shot dead in "row with neighbour over garden hedge"'.[5] The dispute arose in June 2003 over the short length of hedge that ran between their front gardens in Lincoln. The details of the disagreement are not clear. Maybe one neighbour thought it was too high or untidy, or perhaps it spread too far into the other's space. Whatever their differences, they had argued over the hedge for some time, and presumably neither would give an inch – maybe in the name of justice or personal rights. It is alleged that the dispute led to murder. It would be material for a soap opera if only it were not so serious.

Apparently there is a long history of hedge disputes. 'Michael Jones, the honorary life president of Hedgeline, a campaign group seeking legislative control of problem hedges, said: "Passions are aroused with this sort of thing. Disputes can affect people's health, cause stresses and all kinds of tension."'[6]

Should a follower of Jesus react in that sort of way, however 'natural' or 'justified' it might be? If one is going to be passionate, is this the kind of passion to expend energy on? The root cause is a choice to put personal interests first – a bad and ultimately destructive option. Jesus is making a significant case for his followers to be different. The world is evil, the world is violent, the world is unjust; above all, the world is small-minded. And the follower of Jesus needs to know how to respond when violence and injustice touch home. Surely there must be an alternative to the all-too-common passion for rights and revenge that characterizes our society! When all our instincts cry out to hit back, Jesus calls us not to add insult to injury, but to meet evil with good.

Released in 1991 after being held hostage by militants in Beirut for six long years, Terry Anderson stated, 'I am a Christian … it is required of me to forgive no matter how hard that is, and I am determined to do that.' As recorded in the same newspaper editorial, the mother of a murdered girl said of her daughter's killer, 'We have forgiven him. You have to, otherwise it eats into your life and into the lives of those around you.'

The editor's comment affirmed the soundness of Jesus' call to forgive and not to seek revenge:

These words do great honour to the people who spoke them, for they go against the instinctive feelings of anyone who has suffered a terrible wrong. They show a strength of mind and a purity of heart, and they touch all who hear them because they show how goodness is not curdled by the evil done to it.[7]

What a stirring invitation to go beyond the call of duty, beyond the norms of our age, beyond the expectations of all around us! Such attitudes mark out the people of God as different. Be big-hearted; there is more to life than the height of your neighbour's hedge.

'If someone wants to sue you ...'

'And if someone wants to sue you and take your tunic, let him have your cloak as well.'

Here is the perfect antidote to the greed of materialism. In no way is Jesus giving permission for thieves to steal or to benefit from fraud. He is not inviting the world to take advantage of Christians – easy pickings for unscrupulous rogues. That would contradict the whole ethos of biblical law and morality. Nor is it an instruction to us to allow the world to walk all over our legal rights. Jesus is addressing the attitude of God's people in the heart of a greedy world. It's another call to be big-hearted.

The issue of begging is not a simple one. In South Asia I grew accustomed to the existence of beggars; they are a fact of life. But there are beggars and people in desperate need in the streets of London too, and in all our cities. Sometimes that need is as much social or emotional as physical, but the cry for help is no less real. In some cases the need is obvious – in the case of disability, social deprivation, mental ill health or those from violent homes. In other cases they are clearly bogus. I remember watching a young man begging from one bus to the next at a bus stand in Pakistan. Just before entering the bus he carefully twisted the sleeve of his shirt tightly around his arm. Then, bending his arm at a crooked angle, he entered the bus and hobbled down the aisle, to all intents and purposes looking like a cripple with a deformed limb. I didn't give him anything.

I am a soft touch, however, and often do give. I know I have been cheated many times, and have probably been deceived into feeding someone's drug habit or boosting their bank balance. But my philosophy has always been this: it is better to give and to be exploited from time to time than to withhold and to be accused of failing to help someone in need. Of course, we should exercise discernment and not be cheated by criminals and exploiters. But when we meet Jesus on the last day, he will never accuse us of having been too generous.

A big-hearted response to a harsh world is a lifestyle choice. And Jesus urges us to give the benefit of the doubt to the needy.

'If someone forces you to go one mile ...'

'If someone forces you to go one mile, go with him two miles.'

The image comes from the occupying Roman army, which would conscript an unwilling Jew and force him to carry a soldier's equipment. It urges the right response to such unpleasant obligations, over which we have no control. When we have no choice, what should we do? Who is going to be master of our freedom?

Life is full of obligations, whatever we say about freedom of choice and self-fulfilment. A high proportion of everyone's time is spent in doing what we have to do rather than what we want to do. Dreamers dream that the grass is greener on the other side of the hill, and complainers grumble about their poor working conditions or low salaries. In New Testament times many slaves chafed at the bit to gain their liberty, and some are surprised that Jesus did not urge a rebellion or argue for the abolition of the degradation of slavery. Instead, he pointed to a greater way to be free, leaving it to his latter-day disciples to work on the political implications of his gospel. The apostle Paul even had a number of slaves among his spiritual children, and had this instruction for them: 'Slaves, obey your earthly masters with respect and fear, and with sincerity of heart, just as you would obey Christ ... Serve wholeheartedly, as if you were serving the Lord, not men' (Eph. 6:5, 7).

Why did Paul, like his Master, omit to urge the ending of slavery? Because he understood the secret of a greater freedom, an inner freedom for his enslaved converts, more important than the overthrow of social obligations. It is a matter of the heart – the whole heart – willing itself to do what it didn't want to do, and going the extra mile with joy because it was service to Christ.

We likewise have a multiple choice, even when the obligations of life force us to do what we do not want to do. We have the option to respond reluctantly, even angrily or rebelliously, or to bend our wills and respond with a willing heart – or better still, to carry the load an extra mile to prove our absolute control as free people.

Few who have read the books of Pastor Richard Wurmbrand have not been touched by the stories of his years of endurance in prison under the Communists in Romania. I first heard him speak in 1966 when he came to meet an old friend who taught at our Bible college in Devon. His eyes were still sunken and dark-rimmed as a result of his fourteen years of suffering and imprisonment, but they lit up with extraordinary intensity when he began to talk about the memories of his years in solitary confinement. He recounts some of those experiences in his books. 'Alone in my cell, cold, hungry and in rags, I danced for joy every night ... Sometimes I was so filled with joy that I felt I would burst if I did not give it expression.'

Here was a man who had discovered the secret of true freedom, the secret of going the extra mile with joy. 'If a man wills to do everything that he has to do, then he does only the things that he wills – and the hardest trials, being voluntary, become easier.'

When he was finally released after his first eight years in prison, he returned to his family:

They were not expecting me, and I was a fearful sight in my filth and rags. Then I opened the door ... my wife came forward ... When she put her arms around me, I made a great effort and said, 'Before we kiss, I must say something. Don't think I have come from misery to happiness! I've come from the joy of being with Christ in prison to the joy of being with Him in my family.'[8]

No-one can fail to be moved by such insights into the meaning of the true freedom that Jesus planned for all his disciples. It is radical teaching for those who enjoy complaining about the conditions of life. It is an invitation to be master of our circumstances, to be big-hearted and generous in spirit, rather than succumbing to the easier natural tendency to be small-minded and to complain. It is a lifestyle choice.

If someone 'wants to borrow from you ...'

'Give to the one who asks you, and do not turn away from the one who wants to borrow from you.'

Jesus' teaching has come full circle, through byways of spiritual big-heartedness to the material generosity that should distinguish his followers.

How easy it is to run the risk of becoming hardened to the endless appeals that drop through the letterbox or plead with us from the TV screen or from magazines and newspapers. Media manipulators are masters of the heartstrings. Who can resist the appeal of the little girl walking down a lonely corridor, pushing a saline drip stand and holding out a hand to ask for help in her fight against cancer? Or the tragedy of an emaciated little body dying of hunger in Africa, needing only £2 a week to survive? It is media manipulation that tugs at the essential emotions inside us, and we run a high risk of either succumbing (thank God) or becoming cynical and hardened against it.

Jesus had the same tug on his heart as he walked past the lines of beggars, the tear-stained eyes of the cripples, the pathetic cries of the blind and the lame, the grubby faces of the children. How did he handle it all, knowing the extent of the power of which he was capable? There is no evidence that he gave to all who asked, or healed all who came to him (and no evidence that he didn't). He surely exercised discernment, and did not always give what people asked for. Sometimes he provided healing for a broken body, sometimes a word of comfort or acceptance to a person in despair, sometimes time in the midst of a busy schedule, sometimes forgiveness for a tortured soul. Maybe he sometimes gave a few coins to a beggar to meet his need. And, with the advantage of faultless insight, he exercised discernment at all times.

Blessed are the big-hearted

Ken and Katey are very ordinary people in many ways. They used to work with us in Pakistan and spent a year in Karachi following up a large evangelistic campaign we had held. Their life was filled with frustrations but they hung on and did well, eventually returning to teaching in Scotland. But there was an essential restlessness in them that could not be suppressed; and after some years they moved, with their three teenage children, to Romania, where they opened their home to a mixed crowd of street children and people in need.

Let me quote a recent letter from them:

> Our work is going okay, I guess, though so hard at times … I have many days when I feel like giving up, when it all seems too hard and I wonder what I'm doing here. Some of the children we work with are doing well and we see progress in their lives, a desire to change and take the help we offer. Others seem to be going further down. We offer them our hand and they refuse to take it … we have to watch them go further down into the spiral of abuse and pain and there's nothing we can do. At times it's more than I can bear and I wish I could shut myself off, but I can't.
>
> There is one young girl especially who breaks my heart – she's little

and sweet and only twelve, and already has had a life of such pain and hurt that it is hard to imagine. Recently she gave in to the attentions of an older boy who claimed to love her, and had a sexual relationship with him. After this we heard that another older boy had also pushed himself upon her. This young girl never wanted such a life; she wants to go to school and have a family and a life. She poured out her heart to me one day and I cried as she told me she used to plead with God every day to take her life … twelve years old. I know there are millions of such children and at times it overwhelms me.

So that's us … busy, generally happy in a sad sort of way. We have some wonderful friends here, so that helps a lot.

Ken and Katey never had a lot of money to give, but they certainly had a lot of themselves – and a big heart. As Paul said of the Macedonian churches, 'they gave themselves first to the Lord' (2 Cor. 8:5). That sort of generosity is surely not the preserve of the special, but the call of a gracious God to all his people in a world of need. Isn't that what Jesus meant in the Sermon on the Mount?

I am reminded of other friends of mine, who live in Lahore. Ashley is a Pakistani who met his wife when he worked in his own shipping company in Djibouti on the Horn of Africa. It was a time of upheaval in neighbouring Ethiopia and refugees from the civil war were flooding Djibouti. Together Ashley and Seema tried to offer some help and God began to touch their hearts with the needs of the suffering and the poor. They returned to Pakistan and Ashley took a job with a large insurance company.

Then Seema was diagnosed with leukaemia and it seemed that their lives were about to fall apart. 'Every time I looked at Seema to give her encouragement,' Ashley wrote, 'I ended up in tears. Everything looked dark. One month later the doctors advised another series of tests and to our amazement all the tests were clear. It could only be God's answer to our prayers.'

Ashley looks on that year, 1995, as the date he gave his life to Christ. They then began in earnest to open their home to poor children from the street, started a Sunday School and gathered a team to help them in their work among the needy. Every Christmas and Easter they organize a distribution of food and clothing to the poor, and they have opened a charity school to give a good education and a hope in life to children in need. Ashley testifies: 'The words of Jesus in Matthew 25 moved me to tears and I found my life empty without Jesus.' This is what Jesus says in that chapter:

> 'I was hungry and you gave me something to eat, I was thirsty and you gave me something to drink … I needed clothes and you clothed me, I was sick and you looked after me … I tell you the truth, whatever you did for one of the least of these brothers of mine, you did for me' (Matt. 25:35–40).

Ashley and Seema are ordinary people with an ordinary job and a family to raise. Their work with the needy has turned their lives upside down, and they have very little time for their own pleasures or privacy. But they are also a model of big-heartedness and generosity in an often harsh and cruel world. It has been their lifestyle choice.

In the light of the clarity of God's Word and the good that can be achieved by ordinary people making wise choices, how can it be that so many are so reluctant to be big-hearted? It is a mystery we try to plumb in the next chapter.

7

Making excuses

In mid-2001 Eurostar ran a series of advertisements to encourage people to take a day off and go to Paris at a special one-day excursion rate. They proposed several perfect excuses for getting away from the office:

- 'My goldfish died this morning and I am too distraught.'
- 'I can't find my shoes.'
- 'I think I've got 24–hour pneumonia.'
- 'The dog ate my house keys and I need to take him to the vet.'
- 'My leg won't wake up.'

What's your excuse?

Inventiveness knows no bounds when sufficiently motivated. Jesus was aware of fickle human nature and its proneness to make excuses. He told the story of a man who prepared a great banquet and issued the invitations (Luke 14:16–24).

'I have just bought a field,' said one, 'and I must go and see it.'

'I have just bought five yoke of oxen, and I'm on my way to try them out. Please excuse me,' said another.

'I have just got married, so I can't come,' pleaded the third.

Pretty poor excuses, and the warning Jesus gives is that there is no redress for those who choose to miss out on the blessing he has prepared for those who respond on his terms.

The New Testament churches in Macedonia were not rich. Quite the opposite. The apostle Paul refers to their 'extreme poverty' (2 Cor. 8:2). But they were Christians with a sense of dignity and respect. They were not going to be deprived of any blessing just because they couldn't afford it. They had grown up to become a community of generous people who were willing to give whatever they could afford, both to Paul himself and also to others in need. They did not use their poverty as an excuse not to give.

How easy it is to sidestep the call of love and to make excuses, and so miss out on both growing up to maturity and learning the blessing of giving! The New Testament church in Corinth was that kind of church, in striking contrast to the open-hearted Christians in Macedonia. The Corinthians made every excuse in the book to persuade Paul that they were the exception and that they did not need to give for the benefit of the work of God.

We must read between the lines in Paul's letter to the Corinthians in order to discover the excuses they were making. We are not party to the reports Paul had heard from Corinth, but their complaints are obvious from the replies that Paul gave. Let's take a closer look at some of them and see if the Corinthians were able to come up with any acceptable reasons why generosity should not characterize their lifestyle, just as it characterized the Macedonian churches.

1. *I cannot afford to be generous. I can only just get by on my income.*
According to a survey by the Joseph Rowntree Foundation, published in September 2000, a quarter of the population of the United Kingdom 'can be defined as poor because of low incomes

and a lack of essentials'. Essentials, in this context, include a television set, an annual holiday and spare money to decorate the
home. One in four people in Britain cannot afford them. 'It is striking that one in six people in a rich industrialised society perceives
that their income is insufficient to meet the very basic needs
defined by an absolute poverty threshold and that a quarter consider themselves in overall poverty.'[1]

There are many people in Britain today, then, who might well
be justified in saying, 'I cannot afford to give. I can barely survive
on my meagre income.'

It seems that the church in Corinth told the apostle Paul that
they too were in that category – too poor to give away their
precious resources. So Paul told them about another group of
churches, which were no less poor – the Macedonian churches,
including Philippi. In spite of their poverty, said Paul, the
Christians there 'gave as much as they were able, and even beyond
their ability' (2 Cor. 8:3). That is the kind of attitude that honoured
God.

The Macedonians proved that shortage of money was not the
substance of poverty; they did not have a lot to give, but they were
still rich in generosity. They had discovered one of the secrets of
true blessing. Like Ken and Katey, 'they gave themselves first to
the Lord' (2 Cor. 8:5) and then they found it was a privilege to give
away what little they could manage to help others.

A Pakistani pastor whom I knew well provides another shining
illustration of Philippian spirituality. I first met him when he
invited me to speak at an early-morning service he held for poor
brick-kiln workers on the outskirts of Lahore. We met at 5 o'clock
on a dark winter morning. Pastor Otto led the service. I preached
a short message and the gathered men went out into the dark to
another hard day in the poorly paid brickfields. Robert Otto had
no earthly reason to do this work; he was well educated and an
avid reader of serious theology. But he had a passion for the needs
of one of the poorest communities of Christians in his country –
those who live just above the level of serfdom.

In his sixties he had graduated from the bicycle that he had always ridden and now owned a second-hand motorcycle. The last time I met him he was having it repaired. After his death a few months later I came to know more about Pastor Otto's unpretentious lifestyle. He lived in absolute simplicity, and whatever spare cash he had, together with his inheritance, he had given towards the purchase of land on which to build little churches for the Christian brick-kiln workers. Early in his life he had made a lifestyle decision to consider others ahead of himself. A Macedonian Christian indeed!

No doubt he remembered the teaching of the Lord Jesus. One day, Jesus was with his disciples in the temple, watching people putting their gifts into the temple treasury. The rich were filing past and dropping their money into the collecting-box. As they watched, a poor widow came and dropped in two small coins.

'I tell you the truth,' said Jesus, 'this poor widow has put in more than all the others. All these people gave their gifts out of their wealth; but she out of her poverty put in all she had to live on' (Luke 21:1–4).

It is in the heart that God sees the reality of our commitment to him. God does not judge those who can give only a little, nor does he praise those who can give much. But he does expect all of us to give according to what we can afford.

No-one is too poor to be generous. Nowhere in the Bible does God condemn or criticize anyone for being too generous with his or her possessions – not even that poor widow. But often the Bible stands in judgment on those who are greedy and selfish. In God's sight no-one is so poor that they cannot give anything.

2. Let others give the money. I have other gifts to contribute.
The Christians in Corinth were proud that they had been lavishly endued with many spiritual gifts. It was part of their big problem that they loved to display their abilities 'in the Spirit', and everyone had something to contribute. Like peacocks they spread their multi-coloured feathers for the benefit of all. It was quite dazzling.

One gave messages in strange tongues; another set out to interpret the messages; others were gifted with faith, miracles or healing, and so on. They excelled 'in everything – in faith, in speech, in knowledge, in complete earnestness and in your love' (2 Cor. 8:7). As far as it went, it was great.

They thought that was enough. They were spiritually zealous. They knew how to preach and pray and witness to their faith. They thought they had love for one another and for Paul. What more did they need to give?

No, that's not enough, said Paul; 'see that you also excel in this grace of giving' (2 Cor. 8:7). It is good to have lots of spiritual abilities, to be useful in church services, a student of the Scriptures, a person of fervent prayer and able to minister to the needs of others. It is good to exercise the spiritual gifts – but God wants more. Paul said, 'See that you learn how to give your money also. Make sure that you are generous.'

Paul had good reasons for saying this. First, it was a test of authenticity. He wanted to be sure they had the real thing – that their love of gifts and ministry was not just a love of displaying clever abilities, a warped kind of selfishness. 'I want to test the sincerity of your love' (2 Cor. 8:8). Prove that you are truly spiritual people. It is not enough to say that you love unless you demonstrate it with your generosity.

Secondly, he pointed them to the example of Jesus: 'though he was rich, yet for your sakes he became poor, so that you through his poverty might become rich' (2 Cor. 8:9). That is a true model of generosity. Learn the lesson from Jesus!

3. But I am not rich. My gifts will make no difference.
It is both wonderful and intimidating to observe the lavish generosity of the super-wealthy. In 2000 Bill Gates of Microsoft gave away the largest gift of all time when he donated $5 billion through his charitable foundation. Regardless of how the foundation ultimately dispenses the money – and some of it will benefit a lot of underprivileged people – the gesture is magnificent. And it

is said that never in history has there been so much charitable giving as today.

Cynics, of course, always point to the tax benefits, not to mention the ego benefits, of lavish and highly publicized generosity. But such cynicism is misplaced. Whatever motivates the wealthy in their generosity is not our problem. We can just be grateful that the wealth does not remain in the hands of a few, but is spread to benefit the less privileged. A lot of generous giving is clearly wasted on trivia, but some of it does a great deal of good.

It is unfortunate, however, that sometimes these very public super-gifts can be deeply intimidating for those who can manage to give away only a few pounds. In the light of the colossal needs of humanity, what difference can my small contribution make?

No less intimidating is the belief that only First World governments have the resources to make a difference to the massive problems of poverty, international debt and human misery. Thank God that international generosity is on the increase, but very often it, too, is pathetically inadequate. Governments are under public pressure to be seen to be charitable, but the reality is that few governments make more than a token contribution to meeting world need. A few years ago, at the time of floods in India, when the media reported that four million people had lost their homes, the British Government responded with a paltry £250,000. Remember too that much of what is given by the huge corporations is lost in administrative incompetence and corruption.

So never let us see the big and the wealthy as an excuse for withholding our own contribution. The apostle Paul knew that the Corinthians would make this excuse, and he exposed the fallacy. Generosity is not the unique privilege of the wealthy. 'For if the willingness is there, the gift is acceptable according to what one has, not according to what he does not have' (2 Cor. 8:12).

God knows that we cannot give what we do not have. For many pensioners or for those on income support, £20 is a lot of money, whereas others can afford much more. Paul emphasized that it is our willingness to give that God sees, and whatever we can give, whether much or little, is acceptable according to what we can afford. The true value of the gift lies not in what the gift can accomplish, but in the heart of the giver. In any case, if a hundred people give just £10 each, their gifts amount to £1,000. That can make a huge difference and accomplish something significant for God.

See what one elderly Swiss lady wrote to me when she enclosed a small gift for evangelistic work in Pakistan: 'As an old deaconess I have only pocket money. Every month I do send 50 Swiss francs … I would like to be a millionaire to have money for missions. I wish you God's blessing.' Do you think her 50 francs – along with her prayers and God's pleasure – made a difference?

How about this letter from a friend in Wales?

> I enclose a gift of £50 for the work in Pakistan … I am in residential care in the small hospital of the college and recently reached the age of ninety. For nearly sixty years I was a non-salaried worker in the children's home, but since the age of eighty have been entitled to a state pension, my only source of income apart from gracious gifts from the Lord … As the Lord enables me, I support missions in Pakistan and in the Arab World.

Or this, from an elderly lady in Leeds, with £10 enclosed: 'I'd love to send more but can't. The Lord knows – what I give I give to him … God bless you, my dear, and all your fellow workers.'

What grieves God is when he sees that we are unwilling to give – when we cling on to all we can for our own 'needs', and wish we had more to spend on ourselves. That attitude not only grieves God; it also causes him to hold back his blessing.

4. *If I give I will have nothing left for myself!*
Paul evidently tried hard to believe the best about the Corinthians. He had spread the news to other churches about their 'eagerness to help', their 'enthusiasm' to give and 'the generous gift [they] had promised' (2 Cor. 9:1–5). But clearly Paul was trying hard to

believe the best while expecting the worst. Far from being enthusiastic about giving, the Corinthians had made their lifestyle decision and they were now making this final excuse to Paul: 'We won't have enough for ourselves if we give it all away to others!'

Of course, there are limits to generosity and, however needy the world, we help no-one by financially crippling ourselves. But the excuses the Corinthians were making showed up an ugly condition in their lives. And who would suffer the most in the end? The Corinthians. If the Corinthians didn't want to give, they would be hurting only themselves. God does not want reluctant, complaining givers.

Paul was weary of their endless excuses and they led him to issue this warning: 'Remember this: Whoever sows sparingly will also reap sparingly, and whoever sows generously will also reap generously' (2 Cor. 2:6).

The farmer who sows little seed in his field will reap a poor harvest. The farmer who sows plenty of good seed in his field will reap an abundant harvest. This is a matter of common sense. The person who through meanness invests little will also receive little in return. The person who through big-heartedness is generous will also ultimately be truly rich. These rewards are not just pie in the sky. Paul affirms immediate compensation for the generous. This is the subject of another chapter, but we can conclude this section with the two blessings to which Paul pointed the Corinthians – if only they responded positively to his appeal.

First, Paul affirms that 'God loves a *cheerful* giver' (2 Cor. 9:7, italics added). Away with those thoughts that giving is a painful process! Those who give reluctantly out of guilt, or because their arms have been twisted, have got it all wrong. God does not want us to give 'reluctantly or under compulsion' (2 Cor. 9:7). It should be a happy experience – or, as one translation puts it, a 'hilarious' experience – and that is what it will be, when done freely and willingly.

Secondly, God will never allow a generous person to remain poor: '… he who supplies seed to the sower and bread for food will also supply and increase your store of seed and will enlarge the harvest of your righteousness. You will be made rich in every way so that you can be generous on every occasion, and through us your generosity will result in thanksgiving to God' (2 Cor. 9:10–11).

Put aside those excuses. They carry no weight, and God has no category of followers who are excused the privilege of generosity or the blessing of its consequences. That is his word for the cheerful giver, and God keeps his promises!

Now let us take a closer look at some more of the blessings reserved especially for the big-hearted and the generous.

Twelve reasons why we should give

1. God is generous and calls us to imitate him
'Be imitators of God, therefore, as dearly loved children, and live a life of love, just as Christ loved us and gave himself up for us' (Eph. 5:1–2).

2. Jesus Christ commands generosity
'Give to the one who asks you, and do not turn away from the one who wants to borrow from you' (Matt. 5:42).

3. Generosity proves the reality of our love
'If anyone has material possessions and sees his brother in need but has no pity on him, how can the love of God be in him?' (1 John 3:17).

4. Giving is an honour and a privilege
'Entirely on their own, they [the Macedonian churches] urgently pleaded with us for the privilege of sharing in this service to the saints' (2 Cor. 8:3–4).

5. We shall receive if we give
'Give, and it will be given to you. A good measure, pressed down, shaken together and running over, will be poured into your lap' (Luke 6:38).

6. It stores up riches in heaven for us
'Do not store up for yourselves treasures on earth ... But store up for yourselves treasures in heaven' (Matt. 6:19–20).

7. It guarantees us the promise of blessing
'It is more blessed to give than to receive' (Acts 20:35).

8. By giving we are able to support others in times of need
'All the believers were together and had everything in common. Selling their possessions and goods, they gave to anyone as he had need' (Acts 2:44–45).

9. There are so many poor people who need our help
'All they asked was that we should continue to remember the poor' (Gal. 2:10).

10. The church of Christ needs the support of God's people
'The disciples, each according to his ability, decided to provide help for the brothers living in Judea' (Acts 11:29).

11. Christian workers need the financial help of God's people
'... not one church shared with me in the matter of giving and receiving, except you only; for even when I was in Thessalonica, you sent me aid again and again when I was in need' (Phil. 4:15–16).

12. People will be thankful for us and pray for us
'... men will praise God for the obedience that accompanies your confession of the gospel of Christ, and for your generosity in sharing with them and with everyone else' (2 Cor. 9:13).

8

The blessing of giving

I have lost count of the letters that have dropped through my letterbox, personally addressed and assuring me that 'your name, Mr Wakely, has been specially selected (or has successfully passed through to the third round in our draw), and you have been allotted six potentially winning numbers ...' It is an old ploy and we know what follows. 'How would you spend £100,000, Mr Wakely? Take a luxury holiday? Pay off the mortgage? Buy yourself a new car?'

Some people wait in breathless anticipation of that far-off dream becoming a reality, when the winner's cheque will drop through the door and life will change for ever. The lottery has trapped half our population into dreaming dreams of untold happiness, leading to endless frustration, because the dream rarely amounts to anything more than a growing weekly expense. The BBC website once contained this nugget of reality: 'You can see people in any newsagent buying lottery tickets at odds of millions to one and thinking "it could be me", and then buying a packet of cigarettes – with odds of about three to one – and thinking "it won't be me."'

How we deceive ourselves for a little excitement! We love to receive something for nothing – and the next best blessing is to dream about it. But Jesus said, 'It is *more blessed* to give than to receive' (Acts 20:35, italics added).

If it is such a blessing to receive an empty promise, and an even greater blessing to be given a valuable gift, here is a way to get an even greater blessing: to give a gift to someone else. All true Christians should be wanting God's blessing in their lives, and here is a guaranteed way to get it, promised by the Lord Jesus himself.

A lot of people switch their minds off at this point. This is not many people's idea of blessing. This is more like pain than blessing. This chapter has been written to blow the cover on the old lie that blessing is to be found only in opening our hands to receive, and to affirm that God's way to true blessing is quite the opposite – and far more exciting.

Do you want your life to be blessed? Read on.

God's promise to generous people

The boomerang is a remarkable weapon invented by the aboriginal people of Australia, originally for use in hunting. There are several distinct varieties. They are normally flat and bent and made of wood, though there are many other designs for the experts. They can be made of Bakelite, glass or carbon fibre, and they measure 30–75 cm. But the general principle is the same.

Boomerang-throwing is now a highly skilled sport, with national competitions and even a World Cup Championship. The skilled handler holds the boomerang by one end and throws it through the air. It spins as it flies and, if well thrown, will amazingly turn in the air and return to land somewhere close to where it started – or, better still, into the hand of the thrower.

The spinning boomerang can stay in the air for more than a minute – the world record being 1 minute 47 seconds. Unofficially, a boomerang once stayed aloft for 18 minutes before it returned to its thrower. It hit a thermal current and refused to come down. But sooner or later, the sure principle of the boomerang is that, like a loyal dog, it will return to its owner.[1]

God has promised a boomerang to his people. If we learn to give it away, it will not only do its good work, but will then come back to us. Jesus said, 'Give, and it will be given to you. A good measure, pressed down, shaken together and running over, will be poured into your lap' (Luke 6:38).

It is a promise from Jesus that, if we will only begin to practise generosity, we can be sure that we shall receive in return. In fact, he promises that we shall receive even more than we give – in abundance! That is a good investment. Throw away one boomerang; get several in return.

After the Test cricketer C. T. Studd went to China as a missionary in 1885, he inherited a fortune from his father. £29,000 at that time would amount to several million in today's terms. He was a rich man. But Studd also believed that the Bible was true, and, in the words of his biographer, 'he decided to give his entire fortune to Christ, and to take the golden opportunity offered him of doing what the rich young man had failed to do'.[2]

Was he foolish? This was his careful calculation: 'God has promised to give an hundredfold for everything we give to Him. An hundredfold is a wonderful percentage, it is 10,000 percent.'[3]

We must beware making this our dominant motive for giving. It would be foolish to give away our money just because we calculate that God will be obliged to make us even richer. That would be calculated greed. Be assured that God never made C. T. Studd a multi-millionaire after he gave away his fortune, at least not in material terms. The reward came to him in spiritual riches beyond comparison. He not only instigated a mass turning to Christ, especially in the heart of Africa, but also founded one of the great mission societies, which has produced multiple riches for eternity.

Some manipulative evangelists have exploited this teaching to their own material advantage. 'Send me your £100, an investment in eternity, and God will return your gift to you a hundredfold –

guaranteed!' Unscrupulous fundraisers have used all the power of media technique to make gullible people feel that they will become prosperous if they send in all their cash. Some smart operators call it 'seed faith', making it sound like a profitable investment to send money in to them. It is dangerous, deceitful and crooked. Beware!

God does not guarantee an instant return on what we give, or promise how he will reward us. Like the boomerang that got caught in a thermal current, the blessing might take a long time to return to us. But God does make it clear that we can never lose, or be poorer, by giving for his glory. He does guarantee that the return will be greater – far greater – than the sacrifice.

The reward of blessing

There is another incomparable reward for those who are generous, apart from the promise of future return. It is hard to define a 'blessing'. The New Bible Dictionary defines it rather clinically as 'a bestowal of good, usually conceived of as material'. Watchman Nee saw God's blessing as the difference between usefulness and barrenness, the divine touch that rests on the one with whom God is pleased. 'Fruitfulness in the Lord's work is in proportion to his blessing, not in proportion to our limited gifts and power.'[4] Many would prefer to define blessing in terms of the inner contentment that affirms that God is pleased.

It may be hard to define, but it is clear that God has promised blessing to those who are generous. God's blessing was certainly on C. T. Studd when he gave away his fortune. Enclosing a gift of £1,500, he wrote to General Booth of the Salvation Army: 'Hallelujah! We can also thank God by His grace that we have not done this by constraint, but cheerfully and of a ready mind and willing heart.'[5] Another biographer added: 'In reckless extravagance all was placed at the Master's feet. And the Lord was pleased with him.'[6]

There is clearly a definable experience of blessing – the assurance of divine approval and pleasure – in the inner satisfaction and joy of having done good with a significant gift. God's blessing could certainly be read on the face of the old saint in Bilgram in India when he sat back to watch our team devour his family chicken. The blessing of God was clearly evident on the New Testament churches in Macedonia, a community that was addicted to enthusiastic generosity, so much so that they wanted to go on giving far beyond their ability. 'I testify', said Paul, 'that they gave ... beyond their ability ... They urgently pleaded with us for the privilege of sharing in this service to the saints' (2 Cor. 8:2–4). They gave and kept on giving with 'overflowing joy'.

Now here surely is an insight into the motives of some excited people who knew something of the real inner blessing that generosity can bring. The fact that their gift had entailed a sacrifice and had cost them something only increased their joy. 'I will not sacrifice to the LORD my God burnt offerings that cost me nothing,' insisted King David to Araunah, as he gave good money for the oxen he wished to sacrifice as an offering to the Lord (2 Sam. 24:24). He too knew the secret of Philippian generosity: the joy is only increased by the cost of the sacrifice. Would that there were more Philippian churches in the world today!

Those who give for the benefit of others or for the growth of the kingdom of God

- have the joy of sharing in the work of God
- enjoy the inner peace of knowing that they have been obedient to the will of God
- experience the pleasure of seeing their possessions overflow to help people in need and bring joy to people in distress
- have the satisfaction of knowing that their gifts have helped to bring the lost into the kingdom of God
- know the deep, inner contentment of doing something for others that truly expresses Christ's love
- experience the unequalled thrill of going a pure extra mile

for those in need with no personal motive but the honour of
God

These are the marks of authentic Christian love, and the experience of tasting it has no equal. They are just some of the inward
blessings that will come to the heart of the Christian who has
learned to give cheerfully and with enthusiasm.

Rewards in eternity

A rich young man came to Jesus because he wanted salvation.
'Teacher, what good thing must I do to get eternal life?' he asked.
He was not only rich; he was also a very upright Jew who did his
best to keep the commandments. He took his religion very seriously.

Jesus, however, saw that something was standing in the way of
his experiencing true freedom or blessing. There was an idol in his
life, which he had to deal with before he could know the blessing
of salvation. His love of money was preventing him from receiving the promise of eternity. So Jesus challenged him: 'If you want
to be perfect, go, sell your possessions and give to the poor, and
you will have treasure in heaven. Then come, follow me.'

Sadly, the rich young man was unwilling to give away his
wealth. His present prosperity was more important to him than
the promise of treasure in heaven. So he turned his back on Jesus
and 'went away sad, because he had great wealth' (Matt. 19:16–22).

Giving is not a choice for those who wish to follow Christ and
know his blessing. Jesus has *commanded* us to give if we wish to
enjoy our salvation and rewards in eternity. At another time Jesus
said to his disciples, 'Sell your possessions and give to the poor.
Provide purses for yourselves that will not wear out, a treasure in
heaven' (Luke 12:33).

Who can dispute the logic that drove Jim Elliot, the young missionary to the Auca Indians of the Ecuadorean jungle, who was

murdered by the ones he was trying to save? Jim wrote, 'He is no fool who gives what he cannot keep to gain what he cannot lose.'[7]

A reward in heaven is guaranteed to those who have set their hearts on that eternal treasure. 'Do not store up for yourselves treasures on earth … Store up for yourselves treasures in heaven.' The truth is that we cannot take with us into eternity any of our earthly possessions. But we can store up treasure for ourselves in heaven, which will last for ever. We can do this only by being responsible stewards of what we have on earth, and that might well involve giving a lot of it away. That is good advice from Jesus for all who are wise and want infinite profits and an absolutely secure investment.

People will praise God and pray for you

We have already looked at what the apostle Paul said to the Corinthian church about the importance of giving. As he brought his exhortations to them to a close, he added some final comments to encourage them to set out on a generous lifestyle. There are two more blessings that will come as a result of the generosity of God's people.

First, he says that 'men will praise God for the obedience that accompanies your confession of the gospel of Christ, and for your generosity in sharing with them and with everyone else' (2 Cor. 9:13).

It is a strange appeal in the light of Jesus' warnings about those who love the praises of other people more than the praise of God (John 12:43). For sure, we should never give money in order to be seen and praised by others. Jesus clearly condemns ostentatious giving that seeks to be seen and to get us known as generous people. If we are generous, however, people will come to know. Those who receive gifts from us will be grateful to us, and will not only thank us for our kindness but also give praise to God for his provision through us. Paul says that it is good that people should praise God when they see that we are being obedient to his will.

Secondly, 'in their prayers for you their hearts will go out to you, because of the surpassing grace God has given you' (2 Cor. 9:14). Do we want people to pray for us? We can be sure that we shall have many friends who are grateful for our love for them, and who will pray for our welfare, if we have blessed them with our generosity. Paul himself prayed for the church in Philippi because they had generously met his personal needs with their gifts. 'I always pray with joy because of your partnership in the gospel' (Phil. 1:4–5). They had helped him with financial gifts when he was in trouble: 'you sent me aid again and again when I was in need' (Phil. 4:16).

It may seem strange that a person will be made richer by giving things away, but that is literally what the Bible teaches. If we learn the privilege of giving generously to others, we shall never be poorer. The very opposite: by living in obedience to God and becoming a blessing to others, we shall be spiritually richer, happier people, and many will bless God because of us.

9

To whom much has been given

'From everyone who has been given much, much will be demanded; and from the one who has been entrusted with much, much more will be asked' (Luke 12:48).

In chapter 7 I quoted from a *Daily Telegraph* report written under the startling headline: 'One Briton in six claims to be living in poverty.' We can put this into another context.

The UK actually lies tenth – near the top – in the world league table of wealth, and few Britons are poor by the standards of many. Real poverty, according to the report, implies 'severe deprivation of food, safe drinking water, sanitation facilities, health, shelter, education and information'.[1] Britons, even those on income support and living in run-down housing, are privileged in comparison with the citizens of Sierra Leone, where a third of all children die before the age of five. According to a World Health Organisation report published in June 2000,[2] if we had been born in Sierra Leone, we should be doing well to live beyond the age of twenty-six. The average Sierra Leonian dies at the age of twenty-five years and nine months. We should also have the worst access to healthcare, education and income anywhere in the world. It's to be hoped that these statistics will change as the nation slowly recovers from its devastating civil war.

Britons not only have the tenth-highest incomes in the world; they can expect to live to the grand old age of more than seventy-one years because their healthcare and nutrition are excellent. That is longer than the Germans or the Americans.

The legal minimum *hourly* wage in Britain is higher than many Sierra Leonians earn in a *week* – that is, if they can get a job of any kind. Perhaps that is not surprising in the light of the economic breakdown of a country in a state of civil war. But Sierra Leonian wages are actually higher than in Nepal and Bangladesh. Two hours' work in Britain would earn the average weekly wage of a Sudanese or a Haitian. We are a truly privileged people, and this is without beginning to consider the spiritual heritage and wealth of the British Isles. Think for a moment how many evangelical churches there are within walking distance of your home. I guess those who live in the centre of Dartmoor or in the Outer Hebrides might need to walk as far as many Sri Lankans (about 50 miles), but most of us are spoilt for choice. Imagine the situation in a country like Afghanistan!

Stewardship

Where does such privilege place us in the eyes of God? The Bible has much to say in answer to that question and it all comes under the general heading of *stewardship*. Jesus gave a lot of teaching about this, including one especially notorious parable (Luke 16:1–9).

'There was a rich man whose manager [or steward] was accused of wasting his possessions.' Now that was a serious accusation, because if there is one essential requirement in a household manager it is that he should be responsible. If the steward could not be trusted, he should be sacked.

The manager in Jesus' story was no fool, however. He had some fast thinking to do if he was to make good out of a bad scene. He might have lost his job, but he was going to make sure he didn't lose his friends. So, behind his employer's back, he did deals with some of his boss's clients who owed him money. What he did was totally dishonest, and nowhere does Jesus commend him for his dishonesty. But the man was smart, and that is what the master congratulated him for. 'The master commended the dishonest manager because he had acted shrewdly.'

Nevertheless, however smart he was, the day of accounting was sure to come when he would have to answer for his steward-ship. In this story he scored zero for faithfulness and 100% for shrewdness, and he was commended on the day of reckoning for what he did well. Jesus did not dwell on his reward for cheating.

There are three concepts in this story that are helpful to us, and we shall look more closely at each one in turn. They might make a difference to the way we behave. The three lessons are the biblical responses to privilege: *responsibility*, *shrewdness* and *accountability*. And since this story raises such huge questions of honesty, I have added a final section on integrity and faithfulness.

Responsibility

Many years ago I gave some close friends a set of beautiful blue and gold coffee cups that my mother had received as a wedding present in 1937. They might even be valuable, except that two or three of them have been broken and carefully repaired with small steel staples. My friends became stewards of these family heir-looms, and every time we visit they are sure to bring out the old coffee cups after dinner to prove that they are well cared for and that none is missing. Sometimes, to tease them, I suggest that they were just given on loan. But they assure me that they were a gift. It is a small distinction and we are happy for my friends to keep the cups.

Sometimes God reminds us that our life, health and all we possess are ours on loan for as long as the Master pleases. Sometimes we are reminded that we came into the world with nothing, and we shall take nothing with us when we leave. Meanwhile we are responsible for taking care of what has been entrusted to us.

The Bible is full of such reminders. How many of Jesus' parables begin with a king or a man going away to a far country and committing responsibility to his servants? 'Again, it will be like a man going on a journey, who called his servants and entrusted his property to them. To one he gave five talents of money, to another two talents, and to another one talent, each according to his ability' (Matt. 25:14–15).

However we interpret the details of the story, the message is clear. God has given us responsibility on loan, and he expects us to be faithful. We are on probation. It is true of our abilities and natural talents. It is also true of our possessions and our bank accounts, and it is true of our life itself. We are stewards – managers of the Master's property – and stewards are expected to be reliable and responsible. 'Now it is required that those who have been given a trust must prove faithful,' Paul reminds the Corinthians (1 Cor. 4:2).

We do well to learn to look on all that we possess as a trust on loan from a higher authority. Not only is this biblically true; it also helps us to get our material priorities in order. 'Guard the good deposit that was entrusted to you,' says Paul to young Timothy, '– guard it with the help of the Holy Spirit who lives in us' (2 Tim. 1:14).

Shrewdness

Jesus teaches not only responsible management practice but also good business acumen. He is referring not to the City high-flyer but to Mr and Mrs Average in the church pew. The story of the dishonest manager does not sit comfortably with many Christians because of Jesus' failure to condemn sharp and smart practices that seem to fit the marketplace better than the holy closet.

Some friends of mine ran a moderately successful family textile business with good prospects of healthy profits. They were frequently approached by a large company who wished to buy them out, but for the sake of the family the offers were always turned down. Finally, when there was little prospect of continuing the business as a family affair, it seemed right to sell. The next time an approach was made, they put their best negotiator to work to obtain the highest figure possible. The deal they concluded was way beyond their wildest dreams. They sold at exactly the right moment, just before the clothing trade entered a very deep depression.

'In practice,' my friend wrote to me, 'I could see the Lord's hand in it all ... Rather than see myself as streetwise, I see the Lord as being the one whose wisdom was totally dominant.' My friend and his family formed a trust and dedicated their small fortune to help the poor. Their money has touched the lives of thousands with blessing and help. What a fine example!

Nowhere does Jesus commend dishonest practice or the making of money unfairly at another's expense. Corporate fraud belongs in the dirty marketplace and would earn his stern condemnation. Christians in business must be people of the highest integrity, honest and caring in their dealings, but able to cut a good deal and make money. Jesus lays stress on how the shrewd manager should use the good profits he has amassed: the more he gains, the more he is responsible to spend well.

Sadly, Christians often make poor businesspeople because we tend to confuse sharp business practice with greed and profiteering. Jesus knew this only too well: 'the people of this world are more shrewd in dealing with their own kind than are the people of the light' (Luke 16:8). The quality that Jesus commends is the same word as he uses when he tells us to be 'as shrewd as snakes and as innocent as doves' (Matt. 10:16).

Nowhere does Jesus commend folly, carelessness or negligence in financial affairs. The risk-taking of wasteful gambling, whether on the horses, the lottery or in slot machines, is neither shrewd nor (normally) profitable.

Accountability

Every parable on this theme leads up to the inevitable climax: one day we shall all have to give account of our stewardship. The books will be examined. The accounts will be calculated. We shall meet the great Auditor.

If we believed that this world is the only one that matters, that would not be such a problem. Many businesspeople have reaped their rewards and invested their profits in their own honour, with little care for the needs of others. The British countryside is dotted with the great houses and mansions of successful empire-builders of the eighteenth and nineteenth centuries, who wished to perpetuate their own glory and comfort with little expectation of having to give account at the throne of God.

Among the more extraordinary monuments to human folly, the Parliament House in Bucharest, Romania, remains distinctive. In spite of the poverty of the nation, in 1980 Nicolae Ceausescu embarked on plans for a building that would reflect the greatness of his regime. The construction of 'The People's House' required the destruction of some of Bucharest's most elegant nineteenth-century homes and neighbourhoods, together with historic churches, temples and parks. Though still unfinished when Ceausescu was ousted, it is the second-largest building in the world after the Pentagon in Washington DC. 'The whole idea of a 'People's House' came from a man singly determined that Bucharest inspire awe and obedience from his people, from the mind of a man desperately wanting to leave a monument to himself and his power after death.'[3] Nicolae and Elena Ceausescu have had their chance and have now been called to give account of their stewardship. They have left their monuments and investments behind.

It is a mistake to accuse the wealthy of feeding their egos when we all have the same problem, with a greater or lesser degree of success. We feather our nests or save for a rainy day, or just make sure that our designer clothes are better than the neighbours', or that our car is a more recent model. We may not be in a position to build ourselves a palace, but we have a similar problem with our passion for personal significance and recognition.

All of us are accountable for whatever we have done. 'Give an account of your management,' said the rich man in Jesus' parable of the stewards (Luke 16:2). In the parable of the talents, 'After a long time the master of those servants returned and settled accounts with them' (Matt. 25:19).

In my early days in India I was given a daunting task to fulfil. Our mission had purchased a car in Bombay several years earlier, and this was now rotting away in Lucknow, several hundred miles to the north. I went to inspect it. It was a large and ancient Studebaker, quite an unusual car for India, and it had not run on the road for several years. I was to sell it. For some reason, no-one wiser or more experienced was found to do the job and it fell to me alone. When my task was done, I had to give account of what I had achieved and surrender the money I had taken for it, which was to be used to support the work we were doing. I must confess that without that incentive I would probably had given it up as a lost cause.

I shall not recount all the problems I encountered. The first task was to get the car to run; its tyres were flat, its battery dead, the engine rusty. But I didn't give up, and a great day it was when finally it burst into life and I drove a short circuit around a field, proof that it was in running condition. Then I had to find a buyer. Somehow I located someone in the Lucknow bazaar who was willing to pay good money for it. That was the easy part. I then had to effect a legal transfer to the new owner, no small task given that I was not the owner and had no documents to prove that I was acting on the owner's behalf. Furthermore, the car had no up-to-date registration and had been licensed in Bombay, not in Lucknow. Step by step, with many visits to lawyers, to the court and to the vehicle registration office, and with a lot of grace and patience, I overcame the obstacles and collected all the documents. Feeling a sense of real achievement, I delivered the car and its papers to the new owner and he handed over the payment, the largest sum of money I had had in my possession since arriving in India. That night I caught the train to Varanasi, with the cash hidden inside my shirt, to render account of what I had achieved.

A silly illustration, but perhaps it makes the point. The day will come – and we are wise if we keep it constantly in view – when we shall catch the train and face the Great Accountant, in order to answer for what we have accomplished, how we handled our responsibilities and what we did with our resources.

Integrity and faithfulness

Whatever else we may draw from the story Jesus told, we cannot question the high standards of honesty that God requires of his people. Jesus was not suggesting otherwise in underscoring these other virtues. Faithfulness, truthfulness and integrity are essential to the nature of stewardship. Jesus continued to emphasize these values following the story of the shrewd steward:

'Whoever can be trusted with very little can also be trusted with much, and whoever is dishonest with very little will also be dishonest with much. So if you have not been trustworthy in handling worldly wealth, who will trust you with true riches? And if you have not been trustworthy with someone else's property, who will give you property of your own?' (Luke 16:10–12).

It is therefore valuable to remind ourselves that the highest virtue in our stewardship is not to conduct profitable business with our assets or to meet the needs of our unjust world, but to honour the God who has entrusted us with responsibility. And how do we do that? By an absolute commitment to his high principles of integrity and truth. I do not think God would have approved of the methods of Robin Hood, who, according to legend, resorted to robbery and deceit to benefit the poor. How we handle our stewardship is pivotal, and can touch on some difficult ethical issues.

Of course (and this is not only the theme of this book, but a great Christian virtue) we want to be generous. But would it be right to put ourselves into debt in order to give to the needy? My conscience says that in certain circumstances that is all right (in fact, I have done it), on condition we have a clear schedule for repaying the debt. If we cannot see how to repay what we borrow, it probably would be wrong to give away what is not ours.

A simpler dilemma: should we steal from the rich in order to help the poor (the Robin Hood principle)? The answer is clearly no. If I have a debt to be paid and receive an urgent call to help someone in need, what should I do? Should I defer my repayment, exercise my desire to be generous and answer the call for help? Or does the repayment of my debt have a higher claim on my priorities? I have a friend who had borrowed a large sum of money from members of his family to build his home. He then received an unexpected bonus from his work – and immediately bought himself a car. That didn't seem to be a right use of his unexpected wealth and I questioned his priorities. But what if he had given that unexpected bonus to the poor? Would that have been any more justified?

Students face some special dilemmas in these days of student loans that can put them into debt for years. Should a student feel free to give to God's work out of his or her student loan, or would that be a misuse of money given for a different purpose? It is an ethical dilemma. My personal view would be that a student loan is designed to finance the attainment of a qualification, and, since there is a clear schedule for repayment, the student is free to spend it according to his or her judgment, which could well include some generosity. Better to help the needy than to squander it on beer, which is another requirement of many students' budgets. But that is a personal assessment and others may come to a different conclusion. Students may also need to consider the dilemma of debt during a gap year.

One thing is clear. It is vital to resolve the ethical dilemmas and to get into some good and generous budgeting habits while life is still relatively simple. When money suddenly begins to seem plentiful with the first big pay cheque, the risks of losing judgment increase. All too quickly our lifestyles expand to meet the increase in income and we lose our sense of value and the perspectives of a needy world. Good habits and spiritual priorities get easily knocked off course when money becomes available.

These are issues for every individual to grapple with, and a clean conscience and clear commitment to integrity are high priorities. The principles that Jesus endorsed are clear – honesty, integrity, transparency and a commitment to be faithful managers of whatever resources God has entrusted to us.

Before we conclude this chapter, just one word of warning. It is to God and God alone that we are ultimately accountable. Christians can be notoriously judgmental and critical, and we need to beware of pointing fingers at others who appear to be handling their affairs unwisely. Only God knows the secrets of a person's heart, and only he can see what each one is doing with his or her talents. Let us be careful not to play the part of God and to be merciful in our judgments.

10

How to give

Shortly before his crucifixion, Jesus was in the temple in Jerusalem together with his disciples. In a certain area of the great building thirteen large, trumpet-shaped offertory boxes were set up, into which visitors could put their gifts for the work of the temple. Jesus and his disciples sat down one day within sight of the boxes, because he wanted to give his disciples an object lesson (Mark 12: 41–44).

As they watched, some rich worshippers approached and cast their offerings into the containers. It is said that, because the boxes were trumpet-shaped, coins made a distinct ring as they struck the mouths of the boxes – sufficient for the crowd to notice that someone had been magnanimous. Picture the scene: 'Many rich people threw in large amounts', doubtless impressing the common people with their ostentatious philanthropy.

Then the object lesson approached. Not a generous millionaire this time, but a poor widow. Her offering made barely a tinkle on the trumpet-mouth of the collecting-box as she dropped in her 'two very small copper coins'. 'I tell you the truth,' Jesus said to his disciples, 'this poor widow has put more into the treasury than all the others. They all gave out of their wealth; but she, out of her poverty, put in everything – all she had to live on.'

More than all the others? That puts a whole new slant on the meaning of the word 'more'! But Jesus wanted his followers to understand an important truth. The amount of money we are able to give for his work is less important in his eyes than the attitude of heart with which we give. That woman's two small coins (*lepta*) were together worth only a quarter of an *assarion*, the price of two sparrows to offer in sacrifice. In financial terms her contribution would buy only half a sparrow, yet it demonstrated a heart of love and commitment that was pleasing to God. More than all the others! Small resources, maybe – but a big heart.

To be seen by God

God looks on our hearts to examine our motives and to see how much love and generosity is there. That is what will honour him. Our attitude of love to God and to people in need is more important than the amount of money we can give. Attitude is everything to God.

In the Sermon on the Mount Jesus issued a further warning about the danger of giving for the wrong reasons: 'Be careful not to do your "acts of righteousness" before men, to be seen by them ... when you give to the needy, do not announce it with trumpets, as the hypocrites do in the synagogues and on the streets, to be honoured by men' (Matt. 6:1–2).

What a danger! Professional fundraisers use every gimmick in the book to appeal to our egos and to entice us to give more. We might get our name mentioned on television if we donate generously to one of those TV charity appeals. Or it might be inscribed on a plaque or in a book. My own name is inscribed on a brick in the tower of Guildford Cathedral because I once gave half a crown (about 12p) to the cause. Some donors give only in order to get their names into print or to make a reputation for themselves.

But Jesus spoke out strongly against the desire for publicity or ego-feeding: '... when you give to the needy,' he said, 'do not let your left hand know what your right hand is doing, so that your giving may be in secret. Then your Father, who sees what is done in secret, will reward you' (Matt. 6:3–4). That is how to give – secretly, so that only God knows. Then God will reward us in his own inimitable way. That is the kind of honour that true believers should seek.

Hilarious generosity

There is another attitude that delights God. The apostle Paul wrote to the Corinthians in these terms, urging them towards greater generosity: 'Each man should give what he has decided in his heart to give, not reluctantly or under compulsion, for God loves a cheerful giver' (2 Cor. 9:7).

Cheerfulness is not a pious smile while we drop our coins secretly into the collection bag. The word Paul uses is *hilaros*, for what God loves is hilarity in our giving. God is delighted to see people giving in hilarious abandon. In the Greek Psalms the same root word is used for 'to make his face shine' (Ps. 104:15).

I have sat through some church fundraising appeals that seemed more like pulling teeth than inviting people to hilarious enjoyment. I know of some meetings in which the preacher has taken twenty minutes to harangue people to give more and left only ten minutes for the sermon. I have sat through a meeting while a pastor named particular congregation members and told them they could give more – and they had to, or lose face in front of the congregation. That is not what Paul meant when he called for Christians to give cheerfully!

Sacrificial giving

Jesus told the story of a rich man who dressed in purple and fine linen and lived in luxury (Luke 16:19–31). At his gate there was a beggar named Lazarus, 'covered with sores and longing to eat what fell from the rich man's table'.

Jesus told the story to illustrate the point that we reap what we sow. Present prosperity or poverty is no guarantee of our future state, where in glory all wrongs are righted and all injustice is recompensed. But the story carries a secondary meaning – the ugliness of the rich man's treatment of Lazarus.

In reality Lazarus did survive on the crumbs that fell from the rich man's table; he gained his livelihood from the overflow of the rich man's wealth. Without even being aware of it, the rich man shared his surplus with the poor, but it was a miserable offering and it cost him nothing. And, sadly, it reflects much contemporary generosity, which has dispensed with the need for sacrifice.

There can be no true generosity that has cost us nothing. If we give only our excess, the money that is no longer required because all our own needs are already met, the recipient will be grateful, but our offering will be cheap. It is with sacrificial giving that God is pleased.

How much should we give?

No rules are laid down in the Scriptures regarding exactly how much we should give. It is left to everyone's personal conviction. Jesus said that the poor widow gave 'everything – all she had to live on'. Jesus did not condemn her for giving too much. He drew attention to her action not so much as an example to follow but as an attitude to emulate.

In the Old Testament, God's people were commanded to give to God a tithe, or one-tenth, of their income in cash or kind. God told Israel: 'Be sure to set aside a tenth of all that your fields produce each year' (Deut. 14:22). It was given to the priests as their salary and for the expenses of their service in the temple. Giving 10% of their income became the custom for all righteous Jews. The Pharisee whom Jesus exposed as an example of arrogant righteousness boasted, 'I fast twice a week and give a tenth of all I get' (Luke 18:12). Righteous Jews looked on it as their minimum duty to give one-tenth of their income to God. It is certainly not a rigid law for Christians, but it is a very good starting-point.

In our relatively prosperous society, many may be able to give away much more than a tenth of their income. As part of the instruction for the triennial festival gatherings of God's people, Moses taught the Israelites that no-one should come empty-handed. They were to be times of celebration, and each person should decide how much to bring. 'Each of you must bring a gift in proportion to the way the LORD your God has blessed you' (Deut. 16:17).

The example of John Wesley is well known and much quoted, but no less relevant. 'I abridged myself', he wrote in his quaint and dated style, 'of all superfluities, and many that are called necessaries of life.' One biographer wrote this about Wesley's lifestyle: 'When he had an income of thirty pounds a year he lived on twenty-eight, and gave away two. Next year he received sixty pounds, and gave thirty-two in charity. By limiting his expenses to the same sum, he was able to give away sixty-two pounds the third year, and ninety-two the fourth.'[1]

Wesley wrote books and pamphlets that sold in their multiple thousands and made him a very rich man. But his reputation for simple living held, and he continued to live on more or less the same amount as before. As he prospered he was able to give away far more than a tithe. His philosophy on giving is summarized in a sermon on 'the Danger of Riches': '*I gain all I can* without hurting either my soul or my body. *I save all I can*, not willingly wasting anything, not a sheet of paper, not a cup of water … Yet by *giving all I can*, I am effectually secured from "laying up treasures upon earth".'[2]

It is important to reaffirm that there is more to generosity than giving money. Many big-hearted people abound in generous hospitality, providing food and shelter for those in need, or extra-mile effort and long hours of work for the benefit of the needy, with little personal reward. God sees every way in which we provide generously and thoughtfully for those in need.

Purposeful giving

Professional fundraisers know the satisfaction that people derive from feeling that their gift has really accomplished something useful – that it has made a difference in a needy person's life or built something of enduring worth. It is not wrong, in fact it is commendable, to have clear objectives and goals in our giving, as in other aspects of our career.

I have referred to the brick in the tower of Guildford Cathedral that has my initials on it. It was one of the first projects I was involved in, long before I understood anything about giving for the glory of God. It was exciting to watch the red 'thermometer' that was set up to indicate how close we were coming to our target in raising the needed funds for the tower. It gave us something to aim at and a sense of personal achievement as we made our contribution.

The apostle Paul understood all this when he was commissioned to make a collection from the churches in Asia for the relief of the saints affected by famine in Judea (Acts 11:27–29; 1 Cor. 16:1–2). Paul set up a famine fund and toured the churches to promote his project. The collection so caught the imagination of the generous churches in Macedonia that they fell over one another in their zeal to give (2 Cor. 8:1–4). Those in Corinth needed more persuading, but the psychology was clear: Paul presented needs that caught the imagination of the generous, who were then caught up in the thrill of being involved in a project to help their brothers and sisters.

It is a good strategy that encourages enthusiastic giving. We are assailed by multitudes of useful causes that cry out for our generosity. With discernment, it is essential to decide what we want to support, find out how much is needed, and then stretch our faith to make a difference. Enthusiasm in giving grows as we watch the target approach.

It is much easier to give enthusiastically if we feel a sense of ownership of the project, whether we have adopted an orphan in India, feel intimately involved in the fine work of a favourite mission society, contribute to a building or support a national worker. And that enthusiasm can only increase as we see the needed money provided, the project launched and the results coming in to indicate that our money was well spent. Wise is the charity, church or Christian worker who provides good and accurate reports of how our money has been spent and the results of our generosity.

Systematic giving

It is easy to be erratic and disorganized in our giving. When the offering-bag is passed around in the church service – or worse still, the offering-plate – many of us reach into our pockets to see if we can find a few coins in the hope that no-one will see how little we give. In contrast to this kind of carelessness, the apostle Paul taught the Christians in Corinth the importance of giving systematically and regularly. 'Now about the collection for God's people,' he wrote. 'Do what I told the Galatian churches to do. On the first day of every week, each one of you should set aside a sum of money in keeping with his income, saving it up, so that when I come no collections will have to be made' (1 Cor. 16:1–2).

Paul was well organized, and he wanted the Corinthians (and the Galatians, and probably all his churches) to be organized in their giving too. Spontaneous generosity may have its place, but only alongside a steady and systematic pattern of giving.

Where possible, and ideally, regular giving should be a family decision and part of the normal process of family budgeting. It spreads the joy and avoids the tensions that can arise when one partner discovers that the other is giving away too much (or too little). It is better still if the children are involved, so that they can share in the decision-making and partake in a great role-model for their own future. That is so much better than thrusting a few coins into their palms on their way into Sunday school so that they have something to give. In family decision-making each member can feel a sense of commitment to giving and can enjoy the blessing that comes from joint generosity.

11

Who should receive our gifts?

We come now to that most essential and most difficult of tasks: deciding who should be on the receiving end of our generosity. And this is where, of course, I cannot give any specific advice.

There are so many needs for money in the kingdom of God, and all who want to give must make a serious commitment to research and plan where their gifts should go. Haphazard giving is careless and possibly wasteful. Conversely, those who are too meticulous in ensuring that their gifts produce good value for money can find themselves frustrated – and frustrating.

Considerable risk is involved in giving away money. We need to learn to take those risks, calculating them as well as possible, because without them we shall miss meeting some very important needs. During my years working in South Asia I have been constantly assailed by material needs and poverty. One cannot get away from the fact that millions live below the poverty line. A small gift in western terms goes a long way in the Third World, and there is much we can do to help. But without serious discernment much money will be wasted and many will be cheated. I repeat that I am always greatly comforted by the assurance that

God never criticizes the person who gives and is cheated, though he may one day judge the one who doesn't give at all.

There are some guidelines in the Scriptures that shed light on where our money should go. But before we look into them, let me tell an old and familiar story that has greatly helped me in the matter of giving.

The starfish

An old man, walking along the beach at dawn, noticed a young man ahead of him picking up starfish and flinging them into the sea. Catching up with the youth, he asked what he was doing. The answer was that the stranded starfish would die if left until the morning sun came up.

'But the beach goes on for miles, and there are millions of starfish,' exclaimed the old man. 'How can your effort make any difference?'

The young man looked at the starfish in his hand and then threw it to safety in the waves. 'It makes a difference to this one,' he said.

We cannot meet all the world's needs, but we can certainly meet some. Will it make any difference in the end? Of course it will, for those whom we are able to help.

Give to the poor

'If you want to be perfect,' said Jesus to the rich young ruler, 'go, sell your possessions and give to the poor' (Matt. 19:21).

On a recent visit to Pakistan, I went out of my way to meet some extremely poor people. I wanted to talk to some of those who were being helped by a local charity that I support. First among them was Shenaz. Aged about forty, she is illiterate. When her parents died, she had to get work or starve, and she managed to get a job as a cleaner in a private home for a minimum wage.

From the ease of our abundant society it is hard to grasp the implications of absolute poverty: the total absence of the right to life, when survival sometimes depends on a few coins for the next plate of rice, and sickness is the ultimate nightmare. Hopelessness and despair are the daily companions of the truly poor.

Shenaz is married, but her husband has gone out of his mind and wandered away from home. She is left with four children. Their ten-year-old daughter died from food poisoning. Shenaz was unable even to pay rent, and they were thrown out of the house where they had found temporary shelter. Needless to say, the children have never attended school. Shenaz suffers from a thyroid problem, but has no means of seeking treatment. What hope is there for people like her?

Sakina is a widow. Her husband was an electrician, but in the course of his job he was electrocuted and died, leaving Sakina without work and with three sons and three daughters to raise. Sakina had no education and could not read or write. She and her children live in a small, one-room mud house and she sweeps the roads for a pittance. I also met Shanti, another widow. She had fallen from her roof in an accident; she hurt her hand so severely that she can no longer work. Her two sons are drug addicts. They left home and she has no contact with them. I listened to the stories of these women and came away convinced afresh that Christians have an awesome responsibility and much to answer for.

There are millions of such people in the poorer parts of the world. These are the fortunate ones, because they are in contact with Ashley and Seema, the wonderful Christian couple that I referred to in chapter 6, who are trying to help them as best they can. With a little more money much more could be done to bring relief and hope to the desperately poor.

Throughout the Bible God expresses a special concern for the needs of the helpless and the poor. The oppression of the down-trodden was one of the regular themes of the prophets as they denounced injustice and poverty.

'For three sins of Israel,
    even for four, I [the LORD] will not turn back my wrath.

> They sell the righteous for silver,
>   and the needy for a pair of sandals.
> They trample on the heads of the poor
>   as upon the dust of the ground
>   and deny justice to the oppressed.'
> (Amos 2:6–7)

Is it any surprise that one of the marks of the Messiah was that 'The blind receive sight, the lame walk, those who have leprosy are cured, the deaf hear, the dead are raised, and the good news is preached to the poor' (Matt. 11:5–6)?

Jesus regularly paid attention to the needs of the poor and taught his followers to give alms (Luke 12:33) and to remember the poor. His disciples probably gave regularly to beggars out of the common kitty (John 13:29) and Jesus anticipated that they would continue to remember the needs of the poor (Mark 14:7). The early church continued to follow the example that Jesus had set, making collections for the poor and urging compassion on the needy. The apostle Paul repeated to the Galatian church what the apostles had told him to practise: 'that we should continue to remember the poor' (Gal. 2:10).

There are more poor people in the world today than ever in history, and Christian people have a special responsibility to help those in need. That surely must remain a priority in our giving. We may not live in a poor neighbourhood, but everyone lives close to someone who is overwhelmed by needs of one kind or another that they cannot meet. If direct help is difficult, there are numerous organizations that specialize in helping the poor, the orphans and the downtrodden. Here are some guidelines to help us in our giving:

- The Bible indicates that the needs of Christian believers must come first. Paul writes to the Galatians: 'as we have opportunity, let us do good to all people, especially to those who belong to the family of believers' (Gal. 6:10).

- Compassion should always start close to home. Poverty is relative, but there may well be someone whom we know or are close to who is in real need. A gift from us at the right time could be the clearest testimony to the love of God we could ever give. Often half the value of a gift is the expression of thoughtfulness and care that has gone into its giving.

- There are homeless people sleeping in doorways and under arches in all our major cities. In many cases their poverty is the result of some other tragedy in life – a broken home, violent parents or spouse, drugs or other self-abuse – but the end result is the same: a broken life in poverty and need. Thank God for the Salvation Army and other charities that try to help. They need our support both material and physical.

- When disaster strikes, such as illness, theft or natural catastrophe, Christians must be ready to respond compassionately with financial and other help. The faces of the poor and the hurting stare out with numbing regularity from our TV screens and our newspapers. It takes discernment to know where our contributions can make the greatest impact, but we must beware of becoming hardened to human need or cynical of media manipulation.

- Christian charities abound that help the wider world's physically needy, whether through disaster aid, rehabilitation or long-term debt relief. The easiest way we can help the poor is by sending a cheque or signing up to a direct debit to support these charities or to sponsor a child.

- If we are taxpayers we should always be sure to sign a Gift Aid form when sending our gift to a registered charity. In that way, the charity can recover the tax and increase the value of our gift by 28% at current rates.

- Payroll giving can also make the process easier; ask your employer for details.

Beware the platitudes that James referred to: 'Suppose a brother or sister is without clothes and daily food. If one of you says to him,

"Go, I wish you well; keep warm and well fed," but does nothing about his physical needs, what good is it?' (James 2:15–16).

Beware also the easy option, the emotive appeal that may be easy to respond to but whose administrators may not spend the money in the best way. Millions of pounds are raised through excellent and well-organized campaigns such as Children in Need or Red Nose Day. They are targeted at those who wish to give with minimal effort; just pick up the phone and make a credit-card donation. Many such charities are doing a wonderful work and are worthy of support. But, as Christians, we can be more discerning by looking for charities that not only help equally effectively (and often with lower overheads) but also give their aid in the name of Christ and possibly with greater integrity and compassion.

It is worth remembering, too, that physical poverty often has a spiritual solution. The best way to help the materially poor is to bring them to Christ and to introduce them to a caring church community as well as to provide food, clothing and jobs. Spiritual life and human dignity are values no less vital than food in the stomach, good health and hope for tomorrow. Only Christians can fully meet the needs of the world's poor.

It is also important to note that not every well-advertised charity is honest and reliable. Charity abuse and fraud are regularly exposed, and millions of well-meaning people give to 'charities' that are no more than fronts for someone's personal greed. Thank God for the Charity Commissioners, who try to check on the integrity of those who are registered with them. Our own discernment is still essential, however, as we check out the charities to which we should send our valuable gifts.

Give to your own church

Many churches depend on their own congregations for their ministry and the expenses of building upkeep, utilities and salaries. Ensuring that our own church's budget is met should be a high priority in our giving. The first purpose of the Old Testament tithe was to support the priests and the work of the temple. The apostle Paul made a similar claim for local pastors and evangelists in the church: 'If we have sown spiritual seed among you, is it too much if we reap a material harvest from you? ... the Lord has commanded that those who preach the gospel should receive their living from the gospel' (1 Cor. 9:11, 14).

Most churches enable members to give through a regular donor plan, to make a pledge or to pay by direct debit. If we are taxpayers, we should ensure that the church can recover the tax. Churches need to operate on a budget and therefore to know approximately how much their income is likely to be, as this is essential to the good management of any church. All Christians who are committed to a local church fellowship will do well to take an interest in the budget, income and expenditure of their church.

This, of course, requires some careful personal budgeting and forethought. We should think conscientiously how much we can afford to give to support the work of God through our local church, and make a commitment to give regularly. It is the church members who make all the difference in what the church can and cannot accomplish for the kingdom of God.

Give to Christian agencies and missions

The needs of the local church are a priority, but that is just the beginning. The wider work of the church is in the hands of a multitude of fine Christian organizations and individuals who depend on income from other Christians to make a difference in the world.

Of the variety of Christian organizations (and the cries for financial help to meet their objectives) there is no end, and most of them are doing a wonderful and legitimate work that deserves and needs generous support. It is not my duty here to give advice on whom or what to support, but I must make a few comments that may provide guidance to make our money count for God's work.

Give money with discernment

We naturally want our gifts to make a difference. Desiring value for money is good if it means that we want our money to achieve the maximum amount of good. Some giving people insist on supporting only projects that have quantifiable outcomes. If I can give my gift and know that it will provide food and clothing for an orphan for one year, or that it will dig a well to provide clean water for a community, I know exactly what my money has achieved, and that is very satisfying.

In supporting the work of God, greater spiritual discernment is necessary, however, because true value is not always obvious. Money to pay the rent for a training school may be less attractive, but could ultimately be of far greater value; likewise the support of a national evangelist or a subsidy for printing a gospel booklet. Experience shows that many people would prefer to give for a project that is visible (such as a cow for a poor African family) than for something that is invisible (such as an evangelistic outreach campaign). For most receiving agencies, the 'general gift for wherever the need is greatest' is usually the most useful kind. We need to exercise discernment that is able to read beneath the surface. Some of those invisible objectives could transform society and bring results that last for eternity and far outweigh the more appealing but temporal projects.

Eternal values

One does not have to be a Christian to have compassion or to be touched by the sadness of orphans, the hungry, the destitute or street children. Many people of no religious faith have achieved enormous good in many areas of tragedy, and it is wonderful that they do; it is a happy offshoot of a nominally Christian culture. Think of Bob Geldoff and his campaigns for African famine victims; the millions of pounds raised for charities through the BBC's imaginative television appeals; the heroic commitment of Médecins Sans Frontières in some of the world's greatest disaster areas; Project Hope, which transports floating clinics to deprived Third World countries; and the Amy Biehl Foundation, which feeds hundreds of the poor in impoverished South African townships. The world provides endless examples that demonstrate that compassion and care for the needy are not the exclusive preserves of the church. There are a lot of generous people who make no Christian profession at all. In fact, many put the church to shame by their lavish and sacrificial concern.

But there is one area that the non-Christian world cannot touch, and where only Christians can help. It is that area that affects human beings' eternal condition and deepest needs. That is where Christians surely need to target their greatest financial and prayer support.

Missionaries are still urgently needed to preach the gospel, to plant the church and to teach and disciple believers. Every one of them is in need of financial support, however great the sacrifices they are willing to make. Let us not be deceived by the myth that national workers can do the job alone and missionaries are no longer good value for money. National workers also need financial support if the work of the gospel is to be done. And national workers, in general, value the help of their missionary colleagues.

Christian organizations are doing a fantastic work on a shoe-string budget and only Christians can support them in their work for eternity. From provision of the Scriptures to evangelistic campaigns, care of the poor and the high costs of Christian radio – the variety of need is vast and must be high on the priority list for our generous giving.

Remember those far away

It is easy to lavish our gifts on projects and needs that lie close at hand, where we can see their effects and monitor their progress.

Our own community action project or evangelistic mission should be close to the top of our list in our giving, but should never take exclusive possession of our generosity.

The needs far away, out of sight and often out of mind, are usually immeasurably greater than those at home, and therefore equally or more worthy of our generous support. If we were invited to give extragavantly for a £1m building project in our own home church we might accept the responsibility gladly. But we should be careful to get it into balance and not to refuse to make a contribution to build a church in Africa for £10,000 because we cannot afford it. Of course, this is a constant dilemma and a complicated subject, but we must beware of neglecting the needs of the truly needy because we are under pressure to give higher priority to our own needs and luxuries. One church that I know set a great example when they tithed every gift received for their own building project, setting the money aside for church building projects in the Third World.

The joke about the elderly saint who saved her second-hand teabags to send to the missionaries is old and worn, but it contains a tragic element of truth. We are, sadly, prone to ensure that we get the best share before we consider the support of a missionary or a gift towards an overseas project.

The support of missionaries, worthy projects in the developing world, financial help for national workers in poorer countries – these should hold a priority position in the budget of every church and concerned Christian.

Don't forget the small and the hidden
The Christian public is bombarded with cries for help from Christian parachurch organizations, and some of them are as well versed in subtle and attractive fundraising techniques as their secular counterparts. Naturally, the big projects attract the biggest incomes, and the organizations that can afford glossy publications and multi-coloured publicity brochures inserted into Christian magazines are the ones that receive the biggest gifts. And the

costly enterprises that are doing a big job do usually deserve the support and are spending their large incomes well.

As donors, however, let us be careful not to be so enraptured by the gloss and glamour of the big projects that we forget the little ones in our giving. Many of the greatest needs and the finest projects are unassuming or hidden away, with no fundraising mechanism to give glossy presentations and impressive statistics. Sometimes one lonely missionary asking for a few pounds in support gets overlooked in the glare of the big-publicity evangelistic campaign that sets a huge budget. We must be careful to pay special attention to the less attractive, small-budget operations that may spend our money more conscientiously and carefully, with lower overheads, to achieve a more significant result for the kingdom.

Similarly, emergency appeals always attract phenomenal giving from both Christian and non-Christian sources, as long as the emergency is in the spotlight. The latest crisis may not be the wisest place to send our gifts just when the rest of the world is flooding the same need with its generosity – especially if it diverts our gifts from a less prominent but no less desperate need.

Exercise great discernment

In fact, great care and discernment are essential in the jungle of fundraising organizations. Sadly, even Christian missions and evangelistic enterprises do not always operate on the highest principles of integrity. The bigger the budget and the greater the amount of money involved, the greater the temptation to use manipulative techniques to appeal to the generosity of the limited donor base.

I have read the grossly exaggerated reports of some organizations that need large amounts of money to achieve their stated goals. Deceitful statistics, cleverly distorted photography to give impressions of greater results than have really been achieved, exaggerated claims of success – all are used to invite people to part with their money. Then there is the spiritual manipulation performed by those who claim that our gift is a 'seed' from which will sprout greater prosperity and blessing for us.

We need to do a little research into the integrity and track record of some of those who are after our hard-earned cash. Check up on how much the organization will deduct for administrative expenses or further fundraising. Before you send in your cheque or credit-card donation, take care that you are not the victim of manipulative advertising and that you will get an honest report of how your money is spent. Always read the small print. Every word in a fund-raising brochure is significant.

Give to those who are trustworthy

Giving is a privilege and takes far more work than just writing out a cheque. Those who will benefit the most from our gifts are the people who also covet our prayers. And that requires a commitment deeper than mere giving.

The truly generous and big-hearted givers are those who commit themselves to the all-round well-being of the person or project to which they are giving. That demands mutual loyalty and trust – a commitment from both donor and recipient to ensure the glory of God in the accomplishment of his work.

Why not?

Remember this: if we decide we are going to increase our generosity and begin to give some of our money to help others, we can be sure that we shall soon be tempted to keep it for ourselves, to spend it in some other way or to give less. The world, the flesh and the devil (1 John 2:16) are all great tempters to prevent us from becoming generous Christians! Anticipate some of the following threats to your generosity:

- Interest rates may rise and our mortgage payments would go up, not to mention the interest on our bank loan.

- Advertising will tempt us to invest in newer and better models – a computer add-on, satellite TV, a gadget for the car, and so on.
- An economic downturn may make us fear redundancy and dwell on the need to save for that rainy day.
- Private healthcare, extra pension security, life insurance – the invitations to find real peace of mind are endless and costly.
- We feel we are badly in need of a holiday that we had not budgeted for, or we need expensive dental treatment, or the cooker finally breaks down and needs to be replaced.

There are endless reasons why we should spend more on ourselves and so have less to give away. It takes some risk and a huge step of faith to say to ourselves, 'Of course I need this money for myself and can easily justify the expense. But God needs it for his kingdom. There are thousands out there in greater need than I, and he has commanded me to give. Furthermore, God has promised to meet all my needs "according to his glorious riches in Christ Jesus!"' (Phil. 4:19).

Begin to learn the grace and blessing of generosity. Take that step of faith. God will keep his word!

In conclusion

We started with that generous old man in Bilgram, India, who set an example of spontaneous and joyful generosity. He not only modelled big-heartedness; he also modelled Christ-likeness.

When Jesus returns and we have the privilege of meeting him in person, we shall surely discover there is something familiar about that face – not because we have seen his likeness in an art gallery or in a film of his life, but because we have seen him in the faces of those who have walked in his footsteps and chosen his life-style.

> 'Then the King will say to those on his right, 'Come, you who are blessed by my Father; take your inheritance, the kingdom prepared for you since the creation of the world. For I was hungry and you gave me something to eat, I was thirsty and you gave me something to drink, I was a stranger and you invited me in, I needed clothes and you clothed me, I was sick and you looked after me, I was in prison and you came to visit me.'

That is going to be quite a scene. The crowd around us on the King's right hand will be a mixed lot, from every nation, tribe, lan-

guage and people – albeit, by that time, prepared as a bride beauti-
fully dressed for her husband, and thoroughly renewed. And we
shall all be quite confused about what the King is saying:

> 'Lord, when did we see you hungry and feed you, or thirsty and give you
> something to drink? When did we see you a stranger and invite you in,
> or needing clothes and clothe you? When did we see you sick or in prison
> and go to visit you?'

'I tell you the truth,' Jesus will reply as he turns to look at us;
'whatever you did for one of the least of these brothers [and
sisters] of mine, you did for me' (Matt. 25:34–40).

Maybe I shall be able to meet the old man from Bilgram and
thank him for being such an inspiration.

Study guidelines

The following questions have been prepared to provoke discussion in groups or for personal reflection on the issues raised in this book.

1. The heart of a father

1 Are there any figures in your past – ideally your own father, but possibly others – who have modelled fatherhood for you? What good lessons have you drawn from those models? And what false images may you have derived from poor examples of fatherhood, which have even affected your understanding of the nature of God the Father?

2 Describe your understanding of the nature of the Trinity. Was God alone before he began to create? Why did he make the world? Is it biblically true to say that he created because he wished to lavish love on his creation?

3 How do you understand God's generosity? What images immediately come to your mind when you think about God giving gifts to his children (read Eph. 4:8)?

4 Read 2 Timothy 1:8–10. Why was the apostle Paul so

overwhelmed by the grace of God? Should you find God's grace equally overwhelming? And what can be done to increase a sense of wonder in God's generosity?

5 Share together examples of God's generosity that you have personally experienced. What is an adequate response to such a Benefactor?

2. The fruit of the tree

1 Why is it so difficult to accept a totally undeserved gift? Do you have any experiences you can relate that illustrate the difficulty you have had in accepting a gift you did not deserve?

2 Is there any logic in the argument that it is 'immoral and unacceptable' to receive a total and unmerited pardon for crimes committed that deserve punishment? Is it fair that someone who deserves punishment for unspeakable crimes should inherit unspeakable riches? Discuss this unique feature of the Christian gospel.

3 What is the 'catch' in the gospel? When someone receives the free gift of salvation, what is the inevitable consequence?

4 Read the story of the good Samaritan (Luke 10:30–37). When you see someone in need in the street, what is your instant reaction? What was Jesus trying to teach in this story?

5 What evidence do you have that you are a child of God? How do you respond to 1 John 3:14 ? How have you experienced what Paul speaks about in Romans 5:5 ?

3. The dignity of generosity

1 Read Acts 2:42–47. This gives us an insight into the spontaneous nature of the early church. What has changed over the past two millennia? Obviously, some things have

changed for the better. But maybe there are some qualities that the church has lost and should try to recover. Discuss this passage as a model for the church today.

2 *Koinōnia* (fellowship) describes a community that 'has all things in common'. Is true fellowship practicable or possible in the twenty-first century? Some people have reverted to a community lifestyle, not always with great success. What lessons can we learn from New Testament *koinōnia*?

3 'Let us … go on to maturity,' wrote the writer to the Hebrew Christians (Heb. 6:1). What are the marks of a mature Christian? Is it true to say that generosity is a mark of maturity?

4 Is there a place for dignity in Christian behaviour? Or are Christians by definition always beggars in need of help?

4. Lifestyle choices

1 What were your childhood ambitions? How far were you free to follow them? And to what extent have you achieved them? How did your ambitions change when you put your trust in Christ?

2 'Given the choice between reasonable logic and emotional desire, people almost always choose to follow the heart, even if it leads to pain and tragedy.' Is that true? If so, why? As a Christian, how should you make your choices? What will enable you to do the right thing?

3 What convinced Eve that she should taste the fruit? Why was Cain so small-minded? What is the root attitude in your ancestors that should serve as a warning signal to you?

4 Have you ever stood in a sale queue or set your heart on something that required pushing others out of the way to get it? What motivates you at such moments? Is that a 'natural' human instinct for survival? Or is it a carnal reaction that must be crucified? What is the difference between covetousness and a reasonable lifestyle?

5 Is generosity a lifestyle choice? If so, how can it be developed in today's fast-paced, competitive world?

5. Focus and ambition

1 What is the secret of peace of mind? How did the apostle Paul find contentedness? (See Phil. 4:11–12.) The ad-men want us to believe it is to be found in a good insurance policy or an adequate pension. Are they wrong?

2 If it is wrong to 'store up for yourselves treasures on earth' (Matt. 6:19), how can we arrange our affairs so as to take that teaching seriously in today's materialistic age? Should Christians all sell their homes and give away their possessions? Does Jesus glorify poverty? Discuss the implications of Jesus' words for your life today.

3 Discuss the parable of the sower in Luke 8:4–15. Jesus clearly warns against being 'choked by life's worries, riches and pleasures'. How does this speak to you and instruct you in your attitude to advertising, the media and the culture of our day?

4 Debt may not be wrong, but it can become a snare and a curse. What are the godly limits of debt, and how is this teaching relevant to modern society?

5 Are riches and material abundance a mark of God's blessing? Some Christian teaching certainly implies this, and wealth was regarded as a sign of God's blessing on Abraham (Gen. 24:35). How does this teaching square with Jesus' promise, 'Blessed are you who are poor' (Luke 6:20)?

6. Extra-mile living

1 Read Matthew 5:39–39. Express what you find difficult in Jesus' teaching. What can easily be misunderstood or misinterpreted in these verses?

2 To what extent do you think it is godly to stand up for your rights? When should a Christian draw the line in turning the other cheek, going the extra mile and permitting people to take advantage? Is it inevitable that a follower of Jesus will be exploited?

3 Consider Jesus' own life and attitudes. What do you see there of the qualities that he speaks of in these verses? When did he turn the other cheek or go the extra mile?

4 What was Jesus' attitude to beggars? Is there any evidence that he gave money to those who asked him? What else did he give, and to what extent is that a model for us?

5 List what you understand to be the qualities of big-heartedness. Talk about people you know who reflect these values and qualities, and try to learn what it is that makes them the way they are.

7. Making excuses

1 Have you ever made an excuse when the opportunity came to be generous? What was your excuse? How should you have answered or dealt with it?

2 There is much more to giving than donating money. How else can we express generosity in our lifestyle? To what extent may Christians be excused from giving a portion of their money to needy causes?

3 What are the limits of generosity? Read 2 Corinthians 8:1–5. Paul said that the Philippian church gave 'beyond their ability'. Is that honouring to God, or irresponsible? Are there any biblical guidelines on how much Christians should be willing to give?

4 Some organizations say that it is not worth processing small gifts; the cost of the paperwork outweighs the benefits. If you really cannot give enough to make a significant difference to the needs around you, what should you do? Does the Bible give any guidance?

5 Read 2 Corinthians 9:6–11. What does Paul say about the attitude of the Christian who has decided to give? What will be the result of adopting the right attitude?

8. The blessing of giving

1 In what ways have you found that giving is more blessed than receiving?
2 Can you testify to ways in which God has treated your giving as a boomerang and returned more to you than you gave? Is this is a real promise or a realistic expectation? Can we count on it? What form has God's blessing taken in your life?
3 Some smart operators have exploited the good-hearted by promising a great return if we send our money to them. This is sometimes called 'seed faith', 'miracle money' or the 'hundredfold release', and made to look like a good investment. What is wrong with this kind of manipulation?
4 List the blessings that you have received (or would expect to receive) from the Lord as a result of generous giving. Some of those blessings will be immediate and we may expect them on earth; other blessings will be waiting in heaven. List them all.
5 What did the rich young ruler lose when he decided he could not afford to be generous? Read Matthew 19:16–22.

9. To whom much has been given

1 What are the privileges of living in the western world? List them. What responsibilities does that confer upon us, in the light of biblical teaching?
2 What did Jesus mean when he said that his disciples are 'stewards'? Read Luke 12:41–46. Discuss your relationship with the world you live in. Do you believe you have a right to live in it? What are the responsibilities of stewardship?

3 Luke 16:1–9 speaks about the dishonest steward. Why did Jesus commend him? What should we learn from this story with regard to business practice? What qualities does Jesus commend? How can a businessperson be both successful and faithful?

4 What questions do you think the Lord Jesus Christ will ask when one day all his people are gathered before him to give account of what they have done on the earth? List those questions, and then provide your own answers.

10. How to give

1 What differences are there between the way the world motivates people to give and the way the Bible exhorts people to give? List the methods used by the media and the big charities, and comment on how acceptable they are for those who follow the teachings of the Bible.

2 What are the supreme biblical attitudes in generosity? Whether you are appealing for funds or responding to an appeal, what should your attitude be?

3 Discuss biblical teaching on tithing. The Old Testament lays down laws about giving one-tenth of one's income to the priests. Is that a biblical guideline, command or recommendation? What proportion of your income do you think you should consider giving?

4 If you have any experience of good ways to make giving a systematic, successful family event, share it. Have you any hints or tips that might be helpful to others in organizing the way they can give?

11. Who should receive our gifts?

1 Why does God appear to have a bias to the poor? Share together scriptures you have found that indicate God's special concern for the needs of the poor.

2 If we wish to give to the poor, we need to decide how and where to start. Share thoughts on where the poor are to be found in society and any ways you have found of properly addressing their needs. Is it wise to give to beggars? To secular charities? To television appeals?

3 Many churches have expansive and expensive programmes and are always appealing for more money. How can that be balanced with all the other needs that face conscientious Christian people? How high up your list should your own church be?

4 The needs are endless – missionaries, emergency appeals, evangelistic outreaches and worthy Christian societies and projects. How can we discern to whom our money should be given? What guidelines would you propose for the careful and generous giver?

Useful addresses

The following organizations all exist to serve those who wish to give to charities. You may find it helpful to browse the websites or write for more information, as they will open up the world of charities and charitable giving. Not all these organizations are Christian and some of the charities they advertise are of questionable value. In all research discernment is essential, but there is much to be learned. The author welcomes correspondence c/o the publisher.

CharityPortal UK

1 Hoo Cottages
Ledgemore Lane
Great Gaddesden
Hemel Hempstead
Herts HP2 6HF

<www.charityportal.org.uk>

CharityPortal is an excellent introduction to the world of charities. The website lists more than 2,000 UK charities, with some details of their activities and a possibility to give online. It is user-friendly, but it is not Christian and you need to be discerning. But if you want to find out more or wish to donate to a charity, whether for the preservation of hedgehogs or for the Bible Society, this is an easy way to do it.

Charities Direct

Paulton House
8 Shepherdess Walk
London N1 7LB

Tel.: 020 7566 8210
<www.charitiesdirect.com>

CharitiesDirect.com is the home of the National Charities Database, providing regularly updated information on over 10,000 UK charities. Their website provides a database of UK charities, similar to CharityPortal.

Sovereign Giving

32 Highfields Mead
East Hanningfield
Chelmsford CM3 8XA

Tel.: 01245 403197
Email: <info@sogive.com>
<www.sovereign-giving.org.uk>

Sovereign Giving 'specialises in providing a flexible, tax effective service for making donations to charities and churches. Channelling your charitable giving through Sovereign Giving makes your giving simple, flexible and tax effective.'

United Kingdom Evangelization Trust (UKET)

(also known as Stewardship Services)
Oakwood House
Oakwood Hill Industrial Estate
Loughton
Essex IG10 3TZ

Tel.: 020 8502 5600
<www.stewardshipservices.org>

UKET exists 'to maintain and encourage Christian work in a variety of ways through the preaching of the Gospel and the instruction and edification of Christians; services provided by the Trust include Church and Charity Accounts Examination, Insurance, Payroll Services, Charity Administration and Church Trustees & Treasurers Seminars'.

Charities Aid Foundation (CAF)

Kings Hill
West Malling
Kent ME19 4TA

Tel.: 01732 520000
Email: <enquiries@CAFonline.org>
<www.cafonline.org>

CAF is an 'international non-governmental organisation which provides specialist financial services to charities and their supporters. It is committed to increasing the resources of charities worldwide and helping individual and corporate donors add value to their generosity.'

The Giving Campaign

Sixth Floor, Haymarket House
1A Oxendon Street
London SW1Y 4EE

Tel.: 020 7930 3154
Email: <admin@givingcampaign.org.uk>
<www.givingcampaign.org.uk>

The Giving Campaign is 'an independent, national campaign supported by the voluntary sector and the Government. It has been established to increase the amount of money given to UK charities; and, in the long term, to encourage a culture of giving where it is thought natural for everyone able to do so to give money and time to improve the quality of life for others.'

Christians Against Poverty

Jubilee Mill
North Street
Bradford BD1 4EW

Tel.: 01274 760720
Fax: 01274 760745
Email: <info@capuk.org>
<www.capuk.org>

Christians Against Poverty is a national charity, providing debt counselling and financial education to empower people to help themselves out of poverty and be freed from fear, oppression and worry generated by overwhelming debt. The charity operates twenty-nine centres in the United Kingdom.

Further reading

I have hesitated to put together a list for further reading. Giving is something that all Christians should be doing by regular habit, rather than becoming a subject of study. We should beware making ourselves experts on the theology of giving, without at least becoming a stumbling practitioner.

Having said that, here is a list of books that look helpful. Some cover aspects of finance and giving that I have not covered, and that could surely be useful – such as further study in the subject of debt and the theology of Mammon.

Randy Alcorn, *Money, Possessions and Eternity* (Wheaton, IL: Tyndale House, 1989)
An excellent and practical study about money and possessions from a pastor's painstaking study and broad experience.

Craig L. Blomberg, *Neither Poverty nor Riches* (Leicester: Apollos, 2001)
A serious and thorough biblical theology of possessions.

Jim Dunn, *God's Wisdom for Your Money* (Eastbourne: Kingsway, 2002)
This book helps all Christians to get money into perspective and use it wisely by applying biblical principles.

Richard Foster, *Money, Sex and Power* (London: Hodder &
Stoughton, 1985)
This is a classic inspirational study into some of the social
pressures of our day and our spiritual response.

Dayton Howard, *Getting Out of Debt* (Carol Stream, IL: Tyndale
House, 1986)
A financial expert provides practical steps to get out of debt and
create a solid financial base.

Dayton Howard, *Your Money Counts* (Carol Stream, IL: Tyndale
House, 1997)
This book addresses the profound impact that handling money
has on a person's relationship with God.

R.T. Kendall, *The Gift of Giving* (London: Hodder & Stoughton, 1998)
Combining real-life stories with clear biblical teaching, Dr Kendall
explores what it means to tithe.

John MacArthur, *Whose Money is it Anyway?* (Carlisle: STL, 2000)
Enables readers to understand what the Bible really says about
giving and spending.

Stuart Murray, *Beyond Tithing* (Carlisle: Paternoster, 2002)
This book examines the resistance to tithing, its demise and
recovery, and offers possible alternatives.

Brian Rosner, *How to Get Really Rich* (Leicester: IVP, 1999)
Encouragement to learn contentment, share what we have, and
turn our appetites to the pursuit of God.

Ronald J. Sider, *Just Generosity* (Grand Rapids, MI: Baker, 1999)
Encourages believers to care as much about the poor as Jesus did.
It offers a vision for changing both unjust social structures and
the root causes of bad moral choices.

Ronald J. Sider, *Rich Christians in an Age of Hunger* (London: Hodder & Stoughton, 1978)
A classic that tackles the imbalances of poverty and wealth in our world at the turn of a new millennium.

Danny Smith, *Who Says You Can't Change the World?* (Spring Harvest/Authentic Lifestyle, 2003)
This tells the remarkable story of the Jubilee Campaign, a Christian human-rights charity that works to protect the rights of children and families at risk worldwide, and of its sister charity, Jubilee Action, a human-rights pressure group.

Keith Tondeur, *What Christians Should Know about Escaping from Debt* (Tonbridge: Sovereign World, 1999)
Helpful advice for those who want to tackle a big problem.

Keith Tondeur, *What Jesus said about Money and Possessions* (London: Monarch, 1998)
Learning to trust Jesus with our wallets.

Notes

Introduction

1 In 2003, 174 million people. In 1970 it was about 10 million.

1. The heart of a father

1 Adopted and proclaimed by UN General Assembly resolution on 10 December 1948.
2 'He giveth more grace when the burdens grow greater', by Annie Johnson Flint.

2. The fruit of the tree

1 *Christianity Today* editorial by Luís Palau, 1993.
2 Quoted in Richard Collier, *The General Next to God* (Glasgow: Collins, 1965), p. 220.
3 Ibid., p. 223.
4 Ibid.

3. The dignity of generosity

1 John Pollock, *Billy Graham* (London: Hodder & Stoughton, 1966), p. 30.

5. Focus and ambition

1 Figures for 2001–2 from the Department for Work and Pensions, <www.dwp.gov.uk/asd/frs/2001_02/tables/pdf/5_9.pdf>, accessed November 2003.

2 Quoted in John Pollock, *Wesley the Preacher* (Eastbourne: Kingsway, 2000), p. 225.

3 In July 2003 Mr van Hoogstraten's conviction was quashed by the Court of Appeal. He was released from prison in December after the court ruled he could not face a retrial. While claiming that he no longer owns Hamilton Palace, he has also vowed to complete its construction. The saga of his life continues.

4 *The Sunday Telegraph*, 28 July 2002.

5 *The Daily Telegraph*, 23 July 2002.

6 *The Daily Telegraph*, 5 October 2002.

7 <http://news.bbc.co.uk>, 21 May 2003.

8 *The Daily Telegraph*, 9 August 2001.

9 Kenneth Copeland, *Believers' Voice of Victory*, February 2001.

10 Ibid.

11 Recounted by Charles Colson in *Breakpoint*, 6 May 2001.

6. Extra-mile living

1 Geoffrey Moorhouse, *The Missionaries* (London: Eyre Methuen, 1973), p. 160. I owe most of my knowledge of Robert Arthington to this excellent book, with extra material from some web pages.

2 Ibid.

3 In modern terms he would have been a multi-millionaire.

4 Martin Luther, quoted in John Stott, *Christian Counter-Culture: The Message of the Sermon on the Mount* (Leicester: IVP, 1978), p. 108.

5 *The Daily Telegraph*, 15 June 2003.

6 Ibid.

7 *The Daily Telegraph* editorial, 7 December 1991.

8 Richard Wurmbrand, *In God's Underground* (London: W. H. Allen, 1968), pp. 54, 45, 179.

7. Making excuses

1 *The Daily Telegraph*, 11 September 2000.

8. The blessing of giving

1 Information taken from *The Daily Telegraph*, 'Return of a Stone Age Sport' by Gary King, 18 May 2002.

2 Norman Grubb, *C. T. Studd* (London: Lutterworth, 1965), p. 65.

3 Ibid., p. 66. See also Matt. 19:29.

4 Watchman Nee, *Twelve Baskets Full*, vol. 2 (Bombay: GLS, 1973), p. 58.

5 Grubb, *C. T. Studd*, p. 69.

6 Eileen Vincent, *C. T. Studd and Priscilla* (Eastbourne: Kingsway, 1988), p. 79.

7 Elisabeth Elliot, *Shadow of the Almighty* (London: STL, 1979), p. 248.

9. To whom much has been given

1 *The Daily Telegraph*, 11 September 2000.

2 *The Daily Telegraph*, 5 June 2000.

3 From <http://www.rotraveler.com/regionguide/bucharest/
parliamentpalace.php>.

10. **How to give**

1 John Telford, *The Life of John Wesley* (London: Epworth, 1953),
p. 65.
2 John Wesley, *Wesley's Sermons*, vol. 2 (London: John Mason,
1850), p. 124.